First World War
and Army of Occupation
War Diary
France, Belgium and Germany

4 DIVISION
Divisional Troops
Machine Gun Corps
4 Battalion
3 March 1918 - 28 February 1919

WO95/1472/1

The Naval & Military Press Ltd
www.nmarchive.com
Published in association with The National Archives

Published by

The Naval & Military Press Ltd

Unit 10 Ridgewood Industrial Park,

Uckfield, East Sussex,

TN22 5QE England

Tel: +44 (0) 1825 749494

www.naval-military-press.com

www.nmarchive.com

This diary has been reprinted in facsimile from the original. Any imperfections are inevitably reproduced and the quality may fall short of modern type and cartographic standards.

© Crown Copyright
Images reproduced by permission of The National Archives, London, England, 2015.

Contents

Document type	Place/Title	Date From	Date To
Heading	WO95/1472/1		
Heading	BEF 4 Div Troops 4 Battn Machine Gun Corps 1918 Mar-1919 Feb		
Heading	4th Div War Diary 4th Battalion, Machine Gun Corps March 1918		
Heading	War Diary 4th Battn M.G. Corps From 3.3.18 To 31.3.18		
War Diary	In The Field	03/03/1918	31/03/1918
Miscellaneous	4th Battalion Machine Gun Corps No.2	18/03/1918	18/03/1918
Heading	4th Divisional Troops 4th Battalion Machine Gun Corps April 1918		
Heading	War Diary 4th Battn M.G. Corps April 1918		
War Diary	In The Field	01/04/1918	21/04/1918
Operation(al) Order(s)	4th Btn 9 Corps Order No.3		
Operation(al) Order(s)	4th M G Corps Order No.8	09/04/1918	09/04/1918
Miscellaneous	4th Division No.G.S. 162	20/04/1918	20/04/1918
Miscellaneous	Adjt	20/04/1918	20/04/1918
War Diary	In The Field	22/04/1918	30/04/1918
Miscellaneous	To 4th Division "A"	04/06/1918	04/06/1918
War Diary	In The Field	01/05/1918	31/05/1918
Miscellaneous	4th Div.	02/07/1918	02/07/1918
War Diary	In The Field	01/06/1918	30/06/1918
Miscellaneous	To 4th Div.		
War Diary	In The Field	01/07/1918	31/08/1918
Miscellaneous	To 4th Division	05/10/1918	05/10/1918
War Diary	In The Field	01/09/1918	30/09/1918
Miscellaneous	To 4th Division	07/11/1918	07/11/1918
Heading	War Diary of 4th Battalion Machine Gun Corps From 1st October 1918 To 31st October 1918		
War Diary	In The Field	01/10/1918	31/10/1918
Miscellaneous			
Miscellaneous	4th Battalion Machine Gun Corps Instructions For Offence No.2	23/10/1918	23/10/1918
Miscellaneous	4th Battalion Machine Gun Corps Instructions For Offence No.6	28/10/1918	28/10/1918
Miscellaneous	Addendum No.1 To 9th Bn. M.G.C. Instructions For Offence No.6	31/10/1918	31/10/1918
Heading	War Diary of 4th Battalion Machine Gun Corps From Nov 1st 1918 To Nov 30th 1918 (Volume IX)		
War Diary	In The Field	01/11/1918	30/11/1918
Miscellaneous	Casualties November		
Miscellaneous	To 4th Division "A"	05/01/1919	05/01/1919
Heading	4th Battalion Machine Gun Corps War Diary Period December 1st 1918 To December 31st 1918		
War Diary	In The Field	01/12/1918	02/12/1918
War Diary	Valenciennes	03/12/1918	31/12/1918
Miscellaneous	Casualties December 1918		
Heading	4th Battalion Machine Gun Corps War Diary Period January 1st 1919 To January 31st 1919		
War Diary	In The Field	01/01/1919	09/01/1919

War Diary	Anderlues		10/01/1919	31/01/1919
Miscellaneous	Casualties January 1919			
Heading	4th Battalion Machine Gun Corps War Diary February 1919			
War Diary	Anderlues		01/02/1919	28/02/1919
Miscellaneous	Casualties-February 1919			

W3095
1472(1)

BEF

4 DIV TROOPS

4 BATTN MACHINE GUN CORPS

1918 MAR — 1919 FEB

4th Div.

WAR DIARY

4th BATTALION, MACHINE GUN CORPS.

M A R C H

1 9 1 8

Vol II

WAR DIARY

1st Battn. M.G. Corps.

From 3.3.18 to 31.3.18.

Signed EHRoe Lt & Adjt
for Lt. Colonel Commanding

WAR DIARY
or
INTELLIGENCE SUMMARY
(Erase heading not required)

Army Form C. 2118.

Place	Date	Hour	Summary of Events and Information	Remarks and references to Appendices
In the Field	3.3.18		4th Battn. M.G. Corps officially recognized by Division, having been in process of formation since 13.2.18. Lt. Col. W.B. SOMERVILLE, D.S.O. The King's Own Regiment. Commanding: Major R.C. SHIPSTER, M.C. The Manchester Regt. Second in Command.	9MR
	4.3.18		Battalion Training Continued.	9MR
	5.3.18		Battalion practised Test adown & Marched to Assembly positions to be occupied in event of enemy attack. All Companies were en route within 90 minutes of receiving orders to move.	9MR
	6.3.18		Battalion Training Continued	9MR
	7.3.18		" " "	9MR
	8.3.18		" " "	9MR
	9.3.18		" " "	9MR
	10.3.18		" " "	9MR
	11.3.18		" " "	9MR
	12.3.18		" " "	9MR
	13.3.18		" " "	9MR
	14.3.18		Rehearsed for inspection by G.O.C. Division.	9MR

WAR DIARY
or
INTELLIGENCE SUMMARY

(Erase heading not required.)

Army Form C. 2118.

Instructions regarding War Diaries and Intelligence Summaries are contained in F. S. Regs., Part II. and the Staff Manual respectively. Title pages will be prepared in manuscript.

Place	Date	Hour	Summary of Events and Information	Remarks and references to Appendices
In the field	15.3.18		Battalion inspected by G.O.C. Division at the BUTTES DE TIRE. Congratulated on turn out and excellence of march past.	CHR
	16.3.18		Battalion Training continued. Medical inspection of Coys by M.O. CAPT. R.D. HODGSON. The Range and Regt and M.Gc. posted to Command 'A' Coy.	CHR
	17.3.18		Battalion attended Church Parade. Capt T.D. SHERRIFF, M.G.C. posted to Command 'D' Coy. Capt B&H. BENNET, Royal Irish Rifles, relinquishes duties of Adjutant and re-assumes command of 'C' Coy. Lt. E.H. ROSE M.C. The Royal Scots resumes duties of Adjutant.	CHR
	18.3.18		O.C. Coys reconnoitre line preparatory to relief of Guards Divisional M.G. Battn in the GREENLAND HILL, CHEMICAL WORKS and ROEUX Sectors. No motion orders for relief issued.	CHR
	19.3.18		B & C Coys relieve nos 1 & 4 Coys Guards Div. M.G. Battn. Relief successfully carried out.	CHR
	20.3.18		A & D Coys relieve nos 3 & 2 Coys Guards Div. M.G. Battn. Advanced Battn. Hqrs established in FAMPOUX. Battalion details, 8 officers & 314 ORs moved to LOGAN CAMP, ST NICHOLAS, where rear Battn Hqrs are established.	CHR

WAR DIARY
INTELLIGENCE SUMMARY

Army Form C. 2118.

Place	Date	Hour	Summary of Events and Information	Remarks and references to Appendices
In the Field	20.3.18		Battalion Res. 68 guns in or a 3000yds front. Guns manned by half teams only, so as to permit of intermediate reliefs.	BWR
	21.3.18		Heavy shelling of our front & support lines by enemy artillery and T.M.B. Our infantry action followed. Enemy's artillery and improbability of distinguishing signals forced our guns front our S.O.S line. 1 man killed from LOGAN CAMP. Numerous gun positions in line	BWR
	22.3.18		shelled. 8600 rounds expended. Fire teams fired during night by ARRAS Reserve Billets. M.G.s continuable hostile artillery activity on our front but no signs of infantry advance. Enemy parties of enemy seen advancing	BWR
	23.3.18		action 8 N. of the SCARPE. Some excellent shooting was obtained in these targets by few of our guns. Transport and Q.M. Offrs Stores to STUART CAMP. 8 guns (15 withdrawn from line) under LT. T.B. MERRICK M.C. formed into a Reserve Coy. for manning the Army line in case of necessity. Personnel for these guns quartered in Machines at STIRLING CAMP. Old 3 Inch ground line N. of ARRAS dismantled by M.G. Machines	BWR
	24.3.18		Situation still as before. Enemy artillery & aeroplanes very active. Enemy Nunneries S. of Scarpe again successfully engaged by T.Gs. 2600 rounds fired during night on enemy communications.	Retur

Army Form C. 2118.

WAR DIARY
or
INTELLIGENCE SUMMARY.
(Erase heading not required.)

Instructions regarding War Diaries and Intelligence Summaries are contained in F.S. Regs., Part II. and the Staff Manual respectively. Title pages will be prepared in manuscript.

Place	Date	Hour	Summary of Events and Information	Remarks and references to Appendices
3rd Posn	24		Very quiet night. Enemy today S of the SCARPE again largely	CMR.
	25		Situation quiet. Enemy MGs harass our supply	CMR
	26		Good preparations by RMGs trying a raid in our front line in the ROEUX area. Enemy activity causing anxiety in MG defence	CMR
	27		Situation quiet. Advanced Bn. Hqrs moved to CAM VALLEY.	CMR
	28		Situation quiet. After a heavy bombardment commenced at 3 a.m., enemy launched an infantry attack against the Division. But at 6.0 a.m. Enemy made two distinct attacks, he seemed to be about worn. He made slight progress and suffered heavy losses. All things did excellent work in the advancing enemy, being the greater part of their ammunition at close range. Several guns were able to engage on German field batteries coming into action at a range of 1600–2000 yds. By 3 p.m. Infantry with Lewisher a line on our SW of FAMPOUX with a defensive flank along railway to FEUCHY. Bn. Hqrs was established in STIRLING CAMP. Our Casualties were Right, except D Coy, who escaped their casualties as 45. 2/Lt JOYCE + 2/Lt YATES were killed + 2/Lt GOLDEN wounded during the early part of the attack. Withdrawal of guns successfully accomplished	CMR

WAR DIARY
or
INTELLIGENCE SUMMARY.
(Erase heading not required.)

Army Form C. 2118.

Place	Date	Hour	Summary of Events and Information	Remarks and references to Appendices
9th The Jubb	28 (cont)		all Guns firing in new positions before dark. Rations were successfully delivered in spite of uncertainty as to location of Bty H.Qrs. During this action 10 guns & 13 tripods were lost.	BMR
	29.		Situation in line normal. Defence of ARMY LINE organised and general re-distribution of guns.	BMR
	30.		Battn. divided up into groups for ease of control & rationing. Defensive positions of guns & gun pits begun to be made good, also belt boxes and 13 guns ammunition for distribution. Shortage of water in the line is causing it with rations in failure of water points. Water in future to be sent up with rations in petrol tins.	BMR
	31.		Situation in line quiet. Completion of reorganisation of new defence scheme. Total Casualties are as follows:- 2 Officers killed, 1 Officer wounded. 30 ORs killed and 42 ORs wounded. Estimated missing 6 ORs.	BMR

SECRET.   Copy No 78

                4TH BATTALION MACHINE GUN CORPS NO 2.
----

1.   The 4th M.G.Battn Machine Gun Corps will relieve the Guards
   M.G.Battn in the line as follows:-

        B Coy 4th M.G.Battn. relieves No 1 Coy Gds M.G.Battn on 19th inst.
        C "   ditto   No 4 "   ditto   19th inst.
        D "   ditto   No 2 "   ditto   20th inst.
        A "   ditto   No 3 "   ditto   20th inst.

2.   C Company will be relieved in the 3rd System by No 1 Coy
   Guards M.G.Battn. on 19th inst, guides from 2 Sections in 15th Divnl
   Area are to be at Eastern end of FEUCHY H.21.D.9.2. at 3.0 p.m. on
   19th inst.   2 Sections No 1 Coy Guards M.G.Battalion in 3rd
   System 4th Division Area will be under the Command & will be rationed
   by C Company.

3.   Head of B D & A Companies will be at FAMPOUX at 2.0 p.m. on
   the days of releif.

4.   12 Belt boxes per gun & emplacement stores will be taken over,
   copies of receipts for all stores taken over will be sent by Coys to
   Battn. H.Q. within 24 hours of relief.

5.   All other details of releif will be arranged between O's C.
   Companies concerned.

6. ACKNOWLEDGE.

19th March 1918.   P H Rose Lieut & Adjt.
                                                    4th Battn. Machine Gun Corps.

Copies to:- No 1 A Coy
               2 B "
               3 C "
               4 D "
               5 Guards M.G.Battn.
               6 4th Div H.Q.
             8 & 9 Retained.

4th Divisional Troops.

4th BATTALION

MACHINE GUN CORPS

APRIL 1918.

War Diary

4th Battn M G Corps

April 1918

Vol 3

WAR DIARY
or
INTELLIGENCE SUMMARY.
(Erase heading not required.)

Army Form C. 2118.

Instructions regarding War Diaries and Intelligence Summaries are contained in F.S. Regs., Part II. and the Staff Manual respectively. Title pages will be prepared in manuscript.

Place	Date	Hour	Summary of Events and Information	Remarks and references to Appendices
In the Field	1.4.18.		Situation in the line normal with exception of Boars Hotle shelling in SCARPE VALLEY. Our M.Gs continue to engage various small enemy parties, especially S. of Ruin SCARPE.	CHR.
	2.4.18.		About 3.10 am enemy raided a portion of 12th Bde front after a heavy bombardment, and effected an entrance, but was driven out owing to an immediate counter attack. Our guns fired an S.O.S. line and forward guns successfully engaged the enemy as he retired to his own lines. Hostile artillery moderately active through out the day. 15000 rounds harassing fire from our guns during night. During the day gun positions in Nos 4 group were renewed & rest positions selected.	CHR
	3.4.18		Situation normal. Several M.G. gun positions selected. 16000 rounds fired during night on enemy communications.	CHR
	4.4.18		Abnormally quiet day. Hostile artillery practically inactive. Usual harassing fire during night by our machine guns.	CHR

WAR DIARY
or
INTELLIGENCE SUMMARY.

(Erase heading not required.)

Army Form C. 2118.

Place	Date	Hour	Summary of Events and Information	Remarks and references to Appendices
In the field	5/4/18		Heavy gas shelling of our intermediate line during the early morning. Enemy active artillery activity greatly increased during the day. 4000 rounds were fired during night on enemy tracks, and an internal relief in Nos 1, 2 & 3 & 4 gun pits was successfully accomplished.	CHR
	6.4.18		Nothing of any importance to report. Usual harassing fire by our guns during night.	CHR
	7.4.18.		First portion of relief by 1st Canadian M.G. Battn. took place. 16 Teams from forward positions in Nos 3 and 1 & 2 gun pits were relieved & returned to ST NICHOLAS. 3 Officers & 50 ORs reinforcements arrive.	Distributed to Nos CHR
	8.4.18.		16 Teams relieved the previous night proceeded to MARNE CAMP, AGNEZ LES DUISANS. 1st Canadian M.G. Battn. takes over 16 gun positions in Nos 3 & 4 gun relief successfully carried out, though challenged considerably by the extreme darkness of the night. Situation in line normal. The 16 Teams from Nos 3 & 4 gun pits arrive at MARNE CAMP.	CHR
	9.4.18		All new MGs at AGNEZ billeted & refitted.	CHR

WAR DIARY
INTELLIGENCE SUMMARY

Army Form C. 2118.

Place	Date	Hour	Summary of Events and Information	Remarks and references to Appendices
4th & 5th Field Amb	10/4/18		Greatly increased artillery activity throughout the day. Intermediate & Army lines heavily shelled from 10.0 am to 5.0 pm. In spite of this nuisance 10 trams were utilised by 1st Canadian M.B. Battn. and proceeded to MARNE CAMP. Battn. H.Qrs. closed at HARNU & the Railway Cuttings and re-opened at MARNE Camp.	PHR
	11.4.18.		Day spent in bathing, refitting, and cleaning up generally. Battn. warned to be ready to move at 2 hrs notice. All Lewis guns packed & every thing in order. Major W.R. STYLES 18th Regt Grenrs assumes duties of second in command, vice Major G.C. SHIPSTER, attached C.M.G.O. XI Corps.	PHR
	12.4.18.		Division move to LILLERS area, and into the I Corps, 1st Army. Battn. entrained at ABNEZ at 2.0 pm with all guns kit, and arrived at LILLERS about 7.0 pm. Transport proceeding by road arrived at their lines in HAUT RIEUX at 3.0 am. Situation very obscure: A, B, C Coys attached to 10th, 11th & 12th Bdes respectively in Reserve. Battn. H.Qrs. established	PHR

Army Form C. 2118.

WAR DIARY
or
INTELLIGENCE SUMMARY.
(Erase heading not required.)

Instructions regarding War Diaries and Intelligence Summaries are contained in F.S. Regs., Part II. and the Staff Manual respectively. Title pages will be prepared in manuscript.

Places	Date	Hour	Summary of Events and Information	Remarks and references to Appendices
In the Field	12.4.18		At LE PIRE farm, 1 Kilo N.W. of LILLERS	CHR
	13.4.18		A + B Coys take over gun positions from 3rd M.G. Battn. 32 guns on the line, supports being along line of the LA BASSEE canal. C coy at L'ECLEME, and D coy at LE PIRE farm. All in Reserve with 16th Bde.	CHR
	14.4.18		Battn. HQrs move to BAS RIEUX, and advanced HQrs established at BELLERIVE. C Coy take over 18 guns in intermediate positions from 3rd Battn. M.G.C. 8 guns of D coy attached to 11th Bde. 11th Bde attacked enemy positions between ROBECQ and PACAUT WOOD with brigade objective a line running through RIEZ DE VINAGE. This operation was very successful. Enemy counter attacks, objectives being gained at 13.0 were taken. Prisoners stating that they were taken unawares by surprise. B Coy guns went forward with the attacking infantry. 10th Bde attempted an attack on PACAUT wood; A + C coys cooperating. Enemy suddenly shelled the attack before it had fully developed. Supports ran in heavy barrage along the canal and inflicted many casualties. Hostile M.G. and rifle fire was also severe.	CHR
	15.4.18			

WAR DIARY
or
INTELLIGENCE SUMMARY
(Erase heading not required.)

Army Form C. 2118.

Place	Date	Hour	Summary of Events and Information	Remarks and references to Appendices
In the field	15.4.18		Artillery active: Our attack failed to appreciably advance the line, except on the Right (S.W.) side of PACAUT wood, where a post was established with M.G. about 500x beyond original line, in LA RANNERIE Farm—	CWR
	16.4.18		A quiet day. Our M.G.s were able to successfully engage parties of enemy at various times during the day. Our artillery when shelling pieces and farms past drove the enemy out into the open, where our M.G. fire was most effective. Prisoners taken about this time all testify to the unnerving and effects of our M.G. fire. One section of C Coy were able to do a considerable amount of sniping.	PWR
	17.4.18		Considerable increase in hostile artillery fire during the day, especially along CANAL Bank + neighbourhood of HINGES. Our guns again obtained excellent targets on enemy parties. B Coy were relieved by D Coy during the night. Relief was carried out successfully.	PWR

Army Form C. 2118.

WAR DIARY
or
INTELLIGENCE SUMMARY.
(Erase heading not required.)

Place	Date	Hour	Summary of Events and Information	Remarks and references to Appendices
In the field	18/4/18		After a heavy bombardment of the CANAL front, a German plan enemy made a determined attack on the whole Divisional front, with the intention of crossing the LABASSEE CANAL and establishing a line beyond HINGES. The brunt of this attack fell on the 10th Bde, holding the line in front of HINGES, and the enemy succeeded in driving back in line in front of HINGES to the other side of the Canal. A counter attack, however, was established and troops in PACAUT WOOD. Enemy parties seen to have slipped through in pairs and to have been returning near Vladines the Canal ready to fire at Zero. Pioneer detachments were ready to blow up bridges during enforced for the purpose. However, owing to our fire, only one bridge was erected, and all the enemy crossing by this were taken prisoner or made of the attack against RIEZ du VINAGE appears to have been completely held up, and in line in the rectly remained PRISONERS taken in this operation enhanced the as before.	P.R.
			Apparently they did not advance against our M.G. fire. 2 guns lost in this attack, two of them were captured by the enemy	

WAR DIARY
or
INTELLIGENCE SUMMARY.
(Erase heading not required.)

Army Form C. 2118.

Place	Date	Hour	Summary of Events and Information	Remarks and references to Appendices
In the field	18.4.18 (con)		who managed to walk behind them, & got two were damaged by shell fire. The captured guns were without fuses at the time of they got hurt as artillery with them & an infantry escort. They must probably have damaged to escape. Our casualties since the 14th inst as follows: 1 Officer & 70 Ors.	OR
	19.4.18		About 2.45 am small & rather hostile of the enemy were seen approaching in line; the S.O.S signal was sent up. Our enemy were disposed to rifle & M.G. fire before the artillery barrage opened. Considerable hostile artillery activity during the day. CANAL tanks were fairly active. Our M.G.s still getting Canges. HINGES being favourite targets, and teams fire advantage of them. Received excellent targets and columns fire established by all Companies at Dumps of SAA & belt boxes brought up to suitable positions.	OR
	20.4.18		During the early morning 11th Bde attacked enemy positions in PACAUT WOOD. In spite of heavy hostile artillery fire the operation was partially successful, and the line was established [illegible]	OR

WAR DIARY or INTELLIGENCE SUMMARY

Army Form C. 2118.

Place	Date	Hour	Summary of Events and Information	Remarks and references to Appendices
Nt[illegible]	20.6.18 (continued)		in advance of our original positions on both sides of the word. The centre, however, to which it advanced much as before. B Coy lost no guns (damaged by shell fire) in the attack & fired 12000 rounds in support of the infantry advance. During the night the M.G. defence was revised, and the Divisional front divided into four sectors, each under the tactical command of one M.C. Captain. This arrangement has since proved completely satisfactory. Each Coy. has had one complete sector resting at their Coy HQrs, and the men have been given leisure to change clothes, undergo baths & orders.	CMR
	21.6.18		11th Bde continued their attack on PACAUT WOOD at 5.15 am, at 6.0am all objectives were reported taken. Line runs through centre of wood, and the little salient left by Marguise situation has been straightened out. 26 000 rounds were fired by D Coy in support of the attack. An intense relief was successfully carried out during the night, all former teams being relieved.	CMR

4th Bn M.G. Corps order No 3   Secret

1. (a) 1st Canadian M.G. Battn will relieve
8 guns of (Lt MERRICKS) No 2 Group
and 8 guns of (Capt HODGSON's) No 1 group
tonight 7/8 inst.

(b) Guns to be relieved are shewn on the
attached tracing.

2. Guides, under an officer from each group
will meet Canadian M. gun teams at
7.30 pm at following places.
No 1 group guides at railway bridge
H 19 B. 3. 6.
No 2 group guides at railway bridge
at H 14 A. 0. 3.

3. Group commanders will arrange to hand
over 10 full belt boxes of at each gun
position

4. Battery Commander of guns relieving
No 1 group will form his HQ at H 20
D. 2. 9. and will be under orders of OC.
No 1 group until further notice.

4. cont'd —

Battery Commander relieving Lt MERRICK's group will have his HQ at H.16.B.5.7. On completion of relief, Lt MERRICK will hand over teen aiming guns of his group to O.C. No 3 group and will return to LOGAN CAMP.

5. Completion of relief will be notified to Bn. H.Q. by code word SCOTCH.

6. 1 N.C.O. 4 M.G. Bn. will remain at each gun position until midday 8 inst. Section officer 4 M.G. Bn. will also remain until that hour.

7. ACKNOWLEDGE.

Issued at 2 pm

Lt o Adjt
4 Bn. M.G. Corps

SECRET.   Copy No 3
           4th MG Corps Order No 5

1. Remaining guns of No 3 and 4 Group and
   guns of No 5 and 6 group will be
   relieved by 1st Canadian MG Batt tomorrow
   10 inst.
2. Guides at rate of 1 per gun team will
   be at rendezvous arranged by group
   commanders at 5·30 pm
3. 10 full belt boxes per gun in position
   and 8 per gun in reserve will be
   handed over — Also water tins, SAA
   1/a p etc.
4. No 6 group will proceed to AGNEZ by
   march route as soon as relieved.
   Busses to convey personnel of
   remaining groups to AGNEZ have
   been indented for — Details of
   rendezvous will be communicated
   later.
5. Limbers to convey guns etc will be
   arranged as follows:—
       No 1 Group RIFLE CAMP H 24 B 9·7
           3 limbers 7·35 pm
       No 4 Group CROSS ROADS H 13 B 55
           7 limbers 8 pm
       No 5 Group Cross Roads H 13 B 55
           7 limbers 7·30 pm.

Contd

    Batt HQ Cross Roads H 13 B 55
        1 Limber 6.30 pm
    No 6 Group DETAILS CAMP
        2 Limbers 5-30 pm

6. Completion of relief will be reported to Batt HQ.
Batt HQ will close at RAILWAY CUTTING on completion of relief.

9/4/18.

                4° Batt MGC

Copy No 1 to No 1 Group
  " No 2 to No 4 Group
  " No 3 to No 5 Group
  " No 4 to No 6 Group
  " No 5 to Rear HQ
  " No 6 to 1st Canadian MG Batt
  " No 7 File

4th Division No. G.S. 162.

10th Infantry Brigade.   A/Q 4th Divn.
11th Infantry Brigade.   A.D.M.S. 4th Divn.
12th Infantry Brigade.   O.C. Signals.
C.R.A. 4th Divn.   ...P.M. 4th Divn.
C.R.E. 4th Divn.
M.G. Corps.
21st W. York Regt. (P).

During the fighting on the 18th April the Division has once more shown its excellent qualities.

The enemy attacked the Division with at least 7 Battalions in front line; 3 South of PACAUT WOOD; 3 against RIEZ DU VINAGE and 1 or 2 against CARVIN.

Thus the 10th Inf. Bde. were attacked by three Bns and the 12th Inf. Bde. by at least 4.

The previous artillery bombardment was terrific and caused heavy casualities especially in the right Battalion of the 12th Inf. Bde.

Against the 10th Inf. Bde. the enemy was favoured by being able to collect in the wood within a 100 yards of the canal.

The attack /took place in the dark and in spite of all the advantages mentioned above the attack was repulsed with very heavy losses to the enemy. The enemy left 119 prisoners in our hands and a very large number of the enemy were killed. The enemy gained a footing in the Village of RIEZ but was ejected in the evening by a brilliant counter-attack by the 1st Kings Own who had borne the brunt of the attack on the 12th Inf. Bde. during the day.

The attack on the 10th Inf. Bde. front was very severe and fell almost entirely on the 2nd Seaforth Highlanders whose gallantry and determination were magnificent. These were assisted by some men of the Field Companies R.E. who with great skill and courage managed to ferry several of our men across the Canal under fire and materially assisted with their rifles in repelling the attack.

The artillery and the 4th Machine gun Battalion assisted the infantry as usual with all their might, the latter suffering a considerable number of casualities.

The medium trench mortars belonging to the 50th Divn. deserve our warmest thanks for the way they helped to defend the Canal.

H. Hansfath

Lieut-Colonel,
General Staff, 4th Division.

20th April, 1918.
Copy to 50th Div Arty.
 D.T.M.C.

Adjt

Please attach this & similar
documents to his own Diary

 W J U
2/4/18

WAR DIARY
or
INTELLIGENCE SUMMARY.

Army Form C. 2118.

Place	Date	Hour	Summary of Events and Information	Remarks and references to Appendices
In the Field	20.4.18		Enemy artillery very active during the day and evening. HINGES & CANAL heavily shelled, also in two bridges being destroyed. S.O.S. was signalled about 3.30 p.m. and again at 8.20 p.m.; in consequence of the barrage his attempts at infiltrating actions came first in the night, on considerable amount of enemy communications and took place. Our guns also fired during the night in enemy communications and harassing fires during the night. On attached map. Suspicious areas. Present gun positions are shown in attached map.	BHR
	23.4.18		Enemy artillery continued very active during the day. Marked increase in hostile shelling was evident during the evening, & other harassing fire by their artillery. Our M.Gs fired on parties of enemy, especially in PACAUT WOOD, B Coy. replied 3.0 on a party of Germans in front of their position. Harassing fire continued and S.A.A. shots Neuvelaire & forward	
	24.4.18		Hostile artillery lively again, especially near canal and on roads leading to it. RIEZ du VINAGE and HINGES also	BHR

WAR DIARY
or
INTELLIGENCE SUMMARY.
(Erase heading not required.)

Army Form C. 2118.

Place	Date	Hour	Summary of Events and Information	Remarks and references to Appendices
Mill Post	24/4/18 (cont)		Nothing considerable although during the night a considerable number of "rigger" bombs & gas shells were fired by the enemy causing a few slight cases of gas amongst the gun teams. Enemy shelling was Bois de FACHUT showing almost no activity during day, and during the night shelled the area occupied by HQ & Communications. Enemy trench mortar fire during the night. The division was traversed during the night. The division came under Command of XIII Corps at 18:00 hours on this date.	BKR
	25/4/18		Nothing of special interest to report. Hostile artillery as customary. Greatly increased during afternoon. Enemy aeroplane activity the same, high flying & low flying during the three hits of the afternoon. On M.G. emplacement E40 nothing casing & also cannot get the usual harassing fire during the night.	CMR
	26/4/18		3 Station Normal: Enemy trench shelled at intervals during the day, & the bridge over the canal by night. Two raids were successfully carried out during the night as follows:-	

WAR DIARY
INTELLIGENCE SUMMARY

Army Form C. 2118.

Place	Date	Hour	Summary of Events and Information	Remarks and references to Appendices
9,3,7d/W,d/86/A (cont)			A Coy relieved in Right B'de Sector by 3rd Batt M.G.C. 4 guns of 61st Batt M.G.C. in Left B'de Sector relieved by D Coy. Guns of A Coy still manned Anti Aircraft allotted to Experience	CHR
	27/2/18		A considerably quieter day. During the evening A Coy took over Anti Aircraft guns on the Left B'de Sector and D Coy Anti Aircraft Guns accordingly. All Coys have now (guns in the Line) one mg. Coy working at their Coy H/Qrs.	CHR
	28/2/18		Artillery activity more or less normal during the day. Wind whilst & shelling appears to be by calibre and slight concentration. Enemy air activity quite notably the canal bank bridges were the chief and villages & roads behind the lines to considerable amount of our shells lobbed & fired at night. Three very low flying E.A. circled our lines during the afternoon and fired on our infantry.	CHR

W.R. Stepher Major for Lt Colonel
Commanding 4th Battn
Machine Gun Corps

WAR DIARY
or
INTELLIGENCE SUMMARY.

(Erase heading not required.)

Army Form C. 2118.

Instructions regarding War Diaries and Intelligence Summaries are contained in F. S. Regs., Part II. and the Staff Manual respectively. Title pages will be prepared in manuscript.

Place	Date	Hour	Summary of Events and Information	Remarks and references to Appendices
In the field	29.6.18		Hostile artillery activity very much increased. Also vans wind occurred. Shelling of Canal Bank, HINGES, Mt BERNENCHON & on batteries during the day. Enemy snipers are given a great deal of trouble, firing from trees and from behind dead horses. Our apparently lying low and accounted for several of the latter. B Company infantry had an interesting relief during the night. Enemy out an intense artillery & M.G. barrage for heavy Situation in line much as usual.	CHR.
	30.6.18		Shelling of HINGES during afternoon. Our T.Ms successfully meet with a number of suspected hostile sniping posts and caused enemy to considerably abate his energies in that direction. Omagees patrolled helpen successfully. Infantry have shelter available for the Lewis as far as circumstances and material have allowed.	CHR.

**4TH BATTALION,
MACHINE GUN
CORPS.**

No. M.G.C/C 192.
Date.........

TO;- 4th. Division " A "

Herewith original of

War Diary for month of MAY.

[signature]
Lt. Col
Commdg. 4th. Batt.
M.G.C.

4/6/18.

WAR DIARY

INTELLIGENCE SUMMARY.

(Erase heading not required.)

Army Form C. 2118.

W.M.E. Bn. Vol. 4

Place	Date	Hour	Summary of Events and Information	Remarks and references to Appendices
In the field	1/5/18		Quiet day except for short hostile barrage in RIEZ du VINAGE during afternoon. Some gun positions slightly altered to improve fields of fire.	BHR.
	2.5.18.		Enemy artillery intermittently active in back areas, otherwise quiet. Our artillery retaliated on enemy forward positions where he appears to be digging in and wiring.	PHR.
	3.5.18.		Quiet day, though activity in hillsides increased during night.	PHR.
	4.5.18		Heavy hostile barrage in HINGES during early morning. Our back areas shelled during day. Our M.G.s carried out harassing fire during the night in tracks and centres of movement as seen from photographs.	PHR
	5.5.18.		Artillery activity against thrown normal. Our guns fired on PACAUT WOOD during the night.	DHR
	6/5/18		Quiet day. Our guns active against E.A. which were continually seen during daytime. Appreciable amount of harassing fire during night.	PHR

WAR DIARY
or
INTELLIGENCE SUMMARY

(Erase heading not required.)

Army Form C. 2118.

Place	Date	Hour	Summary of Events and Information	Remarks and references to Appendices
In the field	7.5.18		Intermittent shelling during day of CANAL BANK and MT BERNENCHON - LES HARISOINS road. During the night an M.G. carried out the usual harassing fire.	DHR
	8.5.18		Very quiet day. Information from prisoners received of an intended attack on the Corps front, to be made either on 10th or 11th. In view of this information attack was regarded and all preparations made accordingly.	DHR
			Reserve M.G. teams occupied in case of attack. Attack at L'ECLEME marched into line and away with 5 strong firing in the battle position. Lieut. MERRICK M.C. Reserve Bde taken up to Capt. MERRICK M.C. Reserve Bde. Lt. Col. SOMERVILLE D.S.O. appointed Tribunal & Command of 124 I.B. Bde. and MAJ. STYLES assumes command of the Battn.	DHR
	9.5.18		Very quiet day in the line. No sign of hostile infantry activity. W. successfully discharged gas against CORNET MALO during the night, 260 shells cylinders being projected. 64 M.G.s now in line.	DHR
	10.5.18		3 additional guns placed in position first in rear of CANAL, these guns being moved forward by hand for reserve positions in rear.	DHR

Army Form C. 2118.

WAR DIARY
or
INTELLIGENCE SUMMARY.
(Erase heading not required.)

Instructions regarding War Diaries and Intelligence Summaries are contained in F. S. Regs., Part II. and the Staff Manual respectively. Title pages will be prepared in manuscript.

Place	Date	Hour	Summary of Events and Information	Remarks and references to Appendices
In the Field	10.5.18 (cont)		Work continued on shelters for gun teams and ubriqued fields of fire. Hedges & cover etc cut down for this purpose. Gun are a constant source of difficulty in this respect, as it is not thorough effectual to mask fire of guns.	PMR
	11.5.18		Increased artillery activity. RIEZ du VINAGE & CANAL bank shelled intermittently. Enemy thought to be busy digging & wiring his front line; this is confirmed by prisoners statements.	BMR
	12.5.18		Barrying Night arr: new: no attack expected. Reserve Bde Nthnre to Nest Billets. An Aerine positions are invisible. Harrasing fire during night on positions selected & manned.	BMR 4 nds A.A.
	13.5.18		Enemy artillery inspectably active. Chiefly in HINGES and PACAUT WOOD & BMR trenches. Harassing fire was carried out during night on back rounds & MG positions.	PMR.

(A7091) Wt. W12859/M1295 750,000. 1/17. D. D. & L., Ld. Forms/C.2118/14.

WAR DIARY or INTELLIGENCE SUMMARY

Army Form C. 2118.

(Erase heading not required.)

Place	Date	Hour	Summary of Events and Information	Remarks and references to Appendices
In the field	14.5.18		Quiet day. Enemy's artillery active on FITH scale. E.A. active during early morning and evening. Harassing fire on MALO at night on R.152 — CORNET MALO Road. Draft of 20 ORs arrive.	OR
	15.5.18		Quiet. Increased enemy artillery activity, estab. villages of HINGES, MT BERNENCHON, GONNEHEM & BELLERIVE being shelled at intervals & returned night. Our guns very active & mustard gas was used during the night.	OR
	16.5.18		During night harassing CORNET MALO, PACAUT WOOD and suspected of occupied areas. Hostile artillery active in HINGES, RIEZ & BELLERIVE area & returned about mid-night. Our guns opened N.S.O.S. line & did no shelling action Nothing to disturb enemy there. Captain CORNET MALO was bombed during night. Claire K. Hare brought down a Bosch Photographic E.A. in MAGDELENE LOEL H1.E. CAUDRY RVA & observer taken obviously wounded by a gun in Buis Pour des Dunes.	OR

WAR DIARY
INTELLIGENCE SUMMARY
(Erase heading not required.)

Army Form C. 2118.

Place	Date	Hour	Summary of Events and Information	Remarks and references to Appendices
In the field	17.5.18		Unusually quiet day. Our M.Gs harassed enemy communications during the night. E.A. activity ceased during evening and about dusk.	EAR
	18.5.18		Increased artillery activity. HINGES, LES HARISOIRS, BONNEHEM and vicinity being extensively harassed. Our guns fired on Roads & Crossroads during the night.	DnR
	19.5.18		Artillery again active. GONNEHEM, HINGES, LESHARISOIRS, MT. BERNENCHON and CARVIN FARM were subjected to harassing fire. A concentration of mustard gas was fired on LE CAUROY for three quarters of an hour. Our M.Gs carried out harassing fire during the night on CORNET MALO and tracks.	Ears
	20.5.18		Enemy artillery very active harassing back areas day & night. Own artillery also very active harassing with Gas. During the night our M.Gs fired on roads and tracks leading to the enemy's forward areas.	Ears

WAR DIARY
or
INTELLIGENCE SUMMARY.
(Erase heading not required.)

Army Form C. 2118.

Place	Date	Hour	Summary of Events and Information	Remarks and references to Appendices
In the field	21/9/18		Artillery much quieter during the day on both sides. Enemy M.G. activity above normal during the night harassing tracks leading to our front line. Our M.G.O. carried out the usual harassing fire on roads and tracks.	Enc.
	22/9/18		Our back areas fairly heavily bombarded during the night. Mustard Gas, Phosgene and H.E. were used. M.G. activity was normal on both sides. Our guns fired on tracks leading to PACAUT WOOD during the night.	Enc.
	23/9/18		99 Gas cylinders were discharged on N. of PACAUT WOOD. Successfully and our M.G. fired in conjunction. Artillery activity was normal. Our Infantry Patrols gained some useful information with regard to enemy disposition.	Enc.
	24/9/18		Enemy Artillery and M.G. were very active during the day & night. Two of our guns were withdrawn from the CANAL BANK and placed in reserve as Coy HQrs.	Enc.

WAR DIARY
or
INTELLIGENCE SUMMARY.

Army Form C. 2118.

Place	Date	Hour	Summary of Events and Information	Remarks and references to Appendices
In the field.	25/5/18.		Enemy artillery very active. Mt BERNENCHON, BELLERIVE, CENSE LA VALLEE and CANAL BANK were harassed day and night. Concentration of Gas shells were fired frequently, GONNEHEM being heavily shelled for two hours. Our machine guns fired on expected Hostile positions and roads during the night.	Ears.
	26/5/18.		Enemy artillery normal. The CANAL BANK and roads leading to it were heavily shelled at intervals during the evening. Harassing of ration parties. Inabled men fired on during the night by our Guns. Work on positions is progressing favourably and cellars are being reinforced as Quarters for Garrisons and emplacements. A/Col. Somerville D.S.O. assumes Command of the Battalion, after = temporarily commanding the 13th Inf. Bde.	Ears
	27/5/18.		Enemy activity normal. The usual harassing fire being carried out by artillery and M.Gs on both sides. A large number of observation balloons were up and E.A. activity above normal during the day.	Ears
	28/5/18.		Artillery quiet during the day. Increased aerial activity on both sides. Our Guns carried out harassing fire during the night on roads and suspected occupied houses.	Ears

WAR DIARY
or
INTELLIGENCE SUMMARY

Army Form C. 2118.

(Erase heading not required.)

Place	Date	Hour	Summary of Events and Information	Remarks and references to Appendices
In the Field	29/5/18		Increased activity on both sides. The enemy attempted a raid on J/posts but were driven off. E.A. very active all day. Two observation balloons were counted. Enemy artillery harassed HINGES, ROBECQ, LES HARISOIRS, Mt BERNENCHON. Roads day and night. HE and MUSTARD GAS were used. Our guns fired 10,000 rds harassing during the night on enemy roads and tracks.	Can
"	30/5/18		Quieter than previous day. Enemy continues to harass with HE and MUSTARD GAS. Much harassing fire carried out by our guns during the night on enemy communications. The work of clearing away strong cover and hedges to improve fields of fire continues. New positions were selected for some of the guns and emplacements made. Two Officer reinforcements joined the Bn. Enemy.	Can
"	31/5/18		Activity normal. Enemy again used GAS SHE when harassing roads and villages. Our guns fired 13000 rds harassing enemy communications during the night. E.A. activity very marked over our own forward and back areas.	Can

M.G.C/C.470.

To.
4th Div.

Herewith War
Diary for the month
of June.

E A Williams Lt
for. OC 4th Bn.
Machine Gun Corps.

July 2nd 1918

WAR DIARY
INTELLIGENCE SUMMARY.
(Erase heading not required.)

Army Form C. 2118.

4 Bn MG Corps Vol 5

Place	Date	Hour	Summary of Events and Information	Remarks and references to Appendices
In the field	1.6.18	—	Enemy artillery intermittently active during the day, both on forward and support areas. Our guns fired 2500 rounds during the night on "suspected" areas behind the enemy line. A small local attack against an occupied enemy shell hole was undertaken the infantry, with Machine Gun support by A and B Coys, firing from covered positions in the front line.	CHR
	2.6.18		Quiet day. Our guns by night, tracks and batteries selected with considerable attention. Our guns fired 9000 rounds on then harrassing targets during the night.	CHR.
	3.6.18		Another quiet day, except for an occasional shelling of RIEZ du VINAGE & area and Mt BERNENCHON. 6600 rounds fired during the night on enemy tracks & occasional shell holes.	CHR

Army Form C. 2118.

WAR DIARY
or
INTELLIGENCE SUMMARY.
(Erase heading not required.)

Place	Date	Hour	Summary of Events and Information	Remarks and references to Appendices
Inthekeer	4/6/18	—	Enemy artillery carried out its usual harassing fire on CANAL BANK and our communications. Our M.G. fired 10000 rounds during the night.	BMR
	5/6/18	—	Except for a few rounds of gas shell on CANAL BANK and LES HARISOIRS, hostile artillery was almost inactive. Our guns harassed enemy tracks as usual during the night.	BMR
	6/6/18		Enemy artillery again inactive, except for some gas shelling on back areas during the night. One gun fired 900 rounds harassing fire during the night.	BMR
	7/6/18		Gas projected by us during night against enemy positions in PACAUT WOOD, HAUT NIEUPPE FM. in CANAL BANK & MT BERNENCHON. Our guns fired 9500 rounds on enemy communications during the night.	BMR

Army Form C. 2118.

WAR DIARY
or
INTELLIGENCE SUMMARY.
(Erase heading not required.)

Instructions regarding War Diaries and Intelligence Summaries are contained in F.S. Regs., Part II. and the Staff Manual respectively. Title pages will be prepared in manuscript.

Place	Date	Hour	Summary of Events and Information	Remarks and references to Appendices
In the field	8.6.18		Increase hostile activity during day and night at 11.30 pm a barrage of all calibres were put down on our front and support trenches, RIE2 du VINAGE receiving special attention. Our guns fired 19600 rounds in reply to S.O.S. signals. 8600 rounds also fired on enemy harassing targets.	CHR
	9.6.18.		Considerable artillery activity during the night, our front line in the FACAUT & VINAGE sectors being subject to bursts of fire through the night. Our guns fired 14500 rounds in reply. Trench and trench mortar shell dists. on enemy's activity except during night.	CHR
	10.6.18.		Enemy front system was intermittently shelled. Our guns harassed enemy roads and shell holes during the night, firing 8700 rounds.	CHR

(A7092). Wt. W12839/M1293. 75,000. 1/17. D. D. & L., Ltd. Forms/C.2118/14.

WAR DIARY
or
INTELLIGENCE SUMMARY.

Army Form C. 2118.

(Erase heading not required.)

Instructions regarding War Diaries and Intelligence Summaries are contained in F. S. Regs., Part II. and the Staff Manual respectively. Title pages will be prepared in manuscript.

Place	Date	Hour	Summary of Events and Information	Remarks and references to Appendices
Sheikh Zibb	11.6.18		Hostile artillery quiet except for occasional shelling of CANAL BANK. About 12.40 pm our infantry attempted a raid on our regimental shell hole line of our gun catapulted with coverings and flanking fire from the front line. Enemy apparently was expecting this operation and were very alert; afterwards our patrols failed to accomplish its object. Our guns harrassed enemy trades as usual during the night.	EHR
"	12.6.18		Less hostile artillery activity: ROBECQ front system and CANAL BANK lightly shelled at various times during day and night.	EHR
"	13/6/18.		Very quiet during the day. The usual harassing fire was carried out by both sides during the night. At 1.30am a hostile working party was engaged, but rounds were not observed. The work of improving gun positions is progressing steadily.	Ens.

(A7093). Wt. W12839/M1295. 750,000. 1/17. D.D. & L., Ltd. Forms/C.2118/24.

WAR DIARY
or
INTELLIGENCE SUMMARY.
(Erase heading not required.)

Army Form C. 2118.

Place	Date	Hour	Summary of Events and Information	Remarks and references to Appendices
In the Field	14/6/18		Another quiet day. During the night we successfully discharged gas into the N. and S. PACAUT WOOD and the Germans on our right precipitately advanced their lines. 26,500 rounds were fired by C Coy in support of the operations on our right.	Gas.
"	15/6/18		Our guns carried out harrassing fire on enemy communications during the night. Enemy artillery activity moderate during the day. HINGES was heavily shelled at 4pm and 8.30pm. Our guns fired 8,000 rds on enemy communications during the night.	Gas.
"	16/6/18		Enemy artillery activity increased during the day. HINGES, GONNEHEM and CANAL BANK were harrased at different times. Machine guns on both sides were very active. During the night harrassing fire of gas shells was commenced. Our guns supported the day light gas raid by the infantry which was successful. A number of concrete emplacements have been made for the guns and more are under construction. Rose in our line prove satisfactory except for escaping noise made. Experiments are being carried out to devise a means of deading the noise.	Gas.

WAR DIARY
or
INTELLIGENCE SUMMARY.
(Erase heading not required.)

Army Form C. 2118.

Place	Date	Hour	Summary of Events and Information	Remarks and references to Appendices
In the Field	17/6/18		Enemy artillery very active at intervals during the day. CANAL BANK and LES HARISOIRS were heavily bombarded during the night. Gun supports a small infantry raid against some shell hole positions, and carried out the usual harassing fire during the night.	Eau.
"	18/6		Moderately quiet day. Enemy artillery however on consignment during the night. Machine guns on foot rate were active during the night.	Eau.
"	19/6		Very quiet day. M{t} BERNENCHON and RIEZ-DU-VINAGE lightly shelled during the night. Our guns carried out the usual harassing fire.	Eau.
"	20/6		Another very quiet day. Harassing fire as usual during the night. Growing crops are at such a height as to become a serious problem. Large areas have to be cut in order that special patrols may not attract attention. Six tractor mowers have been supplied to assist D Coy in cutting a large area in front of their machine gun	Eau.

Army Form C. 2118.

WAR DIARY
or
INTELLIGENCE SUMMARY.
(Erase heading not required.)

Instructions regarding War Diaries and Intelligence Summaries are contained in F. S. Regs., Part II. and the Staff Manual respectively. Title pages will be prepared in manuscript.

Place	Date	Hour	Summary of Events and Information	Remarks and references to Appendices
In the Field	21/6/18		Hostile activity was slight throughout the day. Our own artillery was fairly active carrying out harassing fire. Our machine guns fired 12000 rounds during the night at enemy communications	Enw.
"	22/6/18		Hostile activity very much below normal. Our guns fired 12000 rounds harassing fire during the night. A "few days" leave to England has been granted to the Battalion and a number of men have gone to hospital. This leave has affected the men at details for more than men on the line.	Enw.
	23/6/18		There was a marked increase in hostile activity in comparison with the previous few days. Enemy aircraft were very active throughout the day. 18 being observed during the day. 10,000 rounds harassing fire were fired on enemy tracks.	Enw.
	24/6/18		Hostile activity again very much below normal. During the day machine guns on both sides were fairly active. Our guns fired 12000 rounds.	Enw.

D. D. & L., London, E.C.
(A8001) Wt. W.1771/M2031 750,000 5/17 Sch. 52 Forms C.2118/14

Army Form C. 2118.

WAR DIARY
or
INTELLIGENCE SUMMARY.
(Erase heading not required.)

Instructions regarding War Diaries and Intelligence Summaries are contained in F. S. Regs., Part II. and the Staff Manual respectively. Title pages will be prepared in manuscript.

Place	Date	Hour	Summary of Events and Information	Remarks and references to Appendices
In the Field	25/6/18		Slight increase in hostile activity but it is still below normal. LES HARISOIRS - CANAL BANK and HINGES were harassed during the night. Our guns carried out the usual harassing fire.	Enc
"	26/6/18		An increased activity as compared with previous days. CANAL BANK and HINGES were fairly heavily shelled during the night. Our guns fired 12,000 rounds harassing fire during the night. A considerable amount of work has been done to improve emplacements and especially strong cubby hole shelters have been built for gun positions. A Sect (1) 21 6/pr joined K Bn.	Excellent
"	27/6/18		300 Gas Drums were projected by us on enemy posts. Gas activity was very active during to-night and the enemy replied by harassing our front as Heavy Machine fire on half side were very active during the night harassing communications.	
"	28/6/18		Our artillery have been very active harassing enemy communications and the enemy replied by short bombardment on our front system. Thousands of the day was very quiet. 1200 rounds were fired by our guns during the night.	Enc

D. D. & L.—London, E.C. (A5003) Wt. W1771/M2031 750,000 5/17 **Sch. 52** Forms C.2118/14

Army Form C. 2118.

WAR DIARY
or
INTELLIGENCE SUMMARY.
(Erase heading not required.)

Instructions regarding War Diaries and Intelligence Summaries are contained in F.S. Regs., Part II. and the Staff Manual respectively. Title pages will be prepared in manuscript.

Place	Date	Hour	Summary of Events and Information	Remarks and references to Appendices
In the Field	29/6/18		Hostile artillery was very quiet during the 24 hours. Our guns fired 13000 rounds harassing enemy communications during the night. Work on gun positions is progressing steadily. They have been generally improved at nearly all positions & shelters for the men have been very much strengthened. A number of "raised slit emplacements" have been built such as guide out posts etc.	Earn.
"	30/6/18		Marked increase in hostile activity after the to long period of quiet. A party of 105 men and 4 Officers of K. R. harassed the Regt. carried out a very successful daylight raid in the morning. The object was to inflict casualties and obtain identification. Three prisoners were taken and about 40 of the enemy killed. 13 of our guns co-operated as follows:- 4 guns of A coy and 3 B Coy fired direct and covered the flanks of the raiding party. 4 guns of B and 4 of C supported the raid by our lead fire. 32000 rounds were fired.	Earn.

SECRET.

W.38.

To 4th Div.

　　Herewith War Diary for the month of July 1918.

　　　　　　　E.A. Williams Lt.
　　　　　　　for.
　　　　　　　LT.-COLONEL.
　　　　　　　COMMANDING 4th BATTN.
　　　　　　　MACHINE GUARDS

WAR DIARY
or
INTELLIGENCE SUMMARY.— 4 Bn M G Coy
(Erase heading not required.)

Army Form C. 2118.

Place	Date	Hour	Summary of Events and Information	Remarks and references to Appendices
In the field	1.7.18		During the day little activity on either side: enemy artillery cannot be issued harassing fire for drafts to rest areas. Our guns harassed enemy tracks and occupied shell holes firing 7000 rounds during the night. Considerable infantry patrol activity. Enemy's own usual night firing programme continued, but still continuing, but a considerable work in cutting crops still remains to be done amount of work in this direction still remains to be done.	BMR
	2.7.18		Very quiet day: usual activity during the night by artillery and our guns on enemy communications. Some slight alteration in our gun positions as follows. 2 guns of A Coy from front line withdrawn to Reserve line: 1 gun of C Coy in front line near PACAUT WOOD moved to extreme right of Divisional sector in BOURNES FARM. 2 guns of B Coy in the snow system moved from PEACOCK FARM to position adjoining to improve field of fire. 4 Anti hill-trans are to be constructed, each to hold 2 guns.	BMR

Army Form C. 2118.

WAR DIARY
or
INTELLIGENCE SUMMARY.
(Erase heading not required.)

Instructions regarding War Diaries and Intelligence Summaries are contained in F. S. Regs., Part II. and the Staff Manual respectively. Title pages will be prepared in manuscript.

Place	Date	Hour	Summary of Events and Information	Remarks and references to Appendices
3.7.K.B. In the field	3.7.18		Nothing of interest to report in the Bn normal front. Our guns harassed enemy shell-holes & communications as usual during the night.	CHR
	4.7.18		A slight increase in artillery activity during the day, the CANAL Bank and HINGES being intermittently harassed. Enemy aircraft more active than usual, especially during the evening. Our guns harassed enemy tracks and roads throughout the night.	CHR
	5.7.18		Quiet day. Enemy gun positions behind by the Naid in the bt hut & Reserve trenches of B Coy are attacked and work begun on the most emplacements. Harassing fire less than usual during the night on account of Patrol activity.	CHR
	6.7.18		At 9.30 am the 2nd Bn Bav. Div. carried out a raid in a front of enemy shell holes E of PACAUT WOOD. 10 guns of C Coy any co-operated, fired 23,000 rounds, 2 guns in position in the front line & 6 guns further down a laneway	CHR

WAR DIARY or INTELLIGENCE SUMMARY.

Army Form C. 2118.

Place	Date	Hour	Summary of Events and Information	Remarks and references to Appendices
In the field	6/8/18 (cont'd)		in rear of the objective; guns of the 3rd Bn. McCuta on the right assisted with rear direct fire. The operation was an entire success. Casualties being inflicted and 3 Mannos Cameliers to the reading party brought back to our lines. No men slightly wounded. Lt. Col. W. Greville proceeds on leave to U.K. Major W.R. Style assumes command of the Batta - during his absence.	DMR
	7/8/18		Very quiet day, but considerable artillery active during the night. RIEZ & Reserve line were shelled fairly heavily and a light harassing hit down in the front line between RIEZ and PACAUT WOOD. Enemy aircraft were more active than usual, flying low over our lines during the evening. Our guns harassed the enemy as usual during the night.	DMR

Army Form C. 2118.

WAR DIARY
or
INTELLIGENCE SUMMARY.
(Erase heading not required.)

Instructions regarding War Diaries and Intelligence Summaries are contained in F. S. Regs., Part II. and the Staff Manual respectively. Title pages will be prepared in manuscript.

Place	Date	Hour	Summary of Events and Information	Remarks and references to Appendices
In the Field	8.7.18		Except for scattered harassing fire during the night, situation very quiet. Our guns fired on CORNET MALO, and enemy tracks & shell holes during the night.	JMR
	9.7.18		Slight increase in hostile artillery activity. MT. BERNENCHON, CANAL BANK and HINGES returning attention during the day. Our guns fired on enemy harassing fire during the night. Lt. Col. North D.S.O. assumed command of the Battalion vice Lt. Col. W SOMERVILLE D.S.O. attached Army Machine Gun Officer X army.	JMR
	10.7.18		Enemy artillery intermittently active. HINGES, BONNE HEM and LOCON area the A/tk VINAGE sector was target. Our patrols were very active & our guns harassed enemy hostile & communication during the night.	JMR
	11.7.18		LES HARRISBOIS and the CANAL BANK was fired on during the day with bursts of M.m shells; desultory harassing fire during the night. Our guns fired 1000 rounds on enemy tracks & shell holes in the Hostile L.s. flying aeroplane was twice active three miles in the Early Morning 3 being seen in a line between 6.45 & 7.30 am.	JMR

WAR DIARY
or
INTELLIGENCE SUMMARY.
(Erase heading not required.)

Army Form C. 2118.

Place	Date	Hour	Summary of Events and Information	Remarks and references to Appendices
In the field	12/9/18		Artillery on both sides was quiet during the day. During the night a little harassing fire was carried out by the enemy on our communications and a few blue cross shells were fired into BELLERIVE. Our machine guns harassed enemy forward communications during the night. A MOIR pill box is being erected in PACAUT WOOD in the SUPPORT LINE. This type is round and built of blocks and can be built up very quickly.	Enc.
"	13/9/18		Enemy activity much greater than on 12th inst. GONNEHEM, the CANAL BANK and our FRONT and SUPPORT LINES were shelled at intervals during the day, and a H.V. gun ranged L'ECLEME with air burst. Four low flying E.A. attempted to cross our lines but were forced to withdraw by our A.A. M.G. fire. 4000 rounds were fired by our machine guns during the night.	Enc.
"	14/9/18		Our Patrols were very active during the evening and night. 8 were sent along the Divisional front. Forward posts have pushed forward and work proceeding to protect them. Enemy artillery rather active – the shelling being scattered over areas and not concentrated on particular points. Enemy aircraft were very active 9 crossed our lines, of these only 2 were low flying. Our machine guns were very active during the night harassing occupied shell holes and tracks.	Enc.

Army Form C. 2118.

WAR DIARY
or
INTELLIGENCE SUMMARY.
(Erase heading not required.)

Instructions regarding War Diaries and Intelligence Summaries are contained in F. S. Regs., Part II. and the Staff Manual respectively. Title pages will be prepared in manuscript.

Place	Date	Hour	Summary of Events and Information	Remarks and references to Appendices
In the Field	15/7/18		Our patrols were again very active and much valuable information gained as to the posts held by the enemy. One patrol engaged an enemy working party 60 strong with good effect killing 1 and wounding 6. Enemy artillery activity has slightly has slightly below normal being confined to intermittent harassing fire. Our machine Guns carried on the usual harassing fire.	Ear.
"	16/7/18		Very Quiet day. Enemy activity generally was below normal. Enemy aircraft however were more active than normal patrolling our lines. 10,000 rounds were fired engaging occupied shell hole and harassing enemy forward Communications.	Ear
"	17/7/18		During the day enemy artillery was very quiet but became more active during the evening and night. Support and reserve lines in VINAGE SECTOR, LES HARISOIRS, Hd CANAL BANK and BLACKFRIARS Bridge being shelled at intervals during the night. Enemy machine Guns were very active during the night however trench Our machine Guns were also very active.	Ear

WAR DIARY or INTELLIGENCE SUMMARY

Army Form C. 2118.

Place	Date	Hour	Summary of Events and Information	Remarks and references to Appendices
In the Field	18/3/18		A very successful raid was carried out by the 2/7 Bn Duke of Wellington's Regt against the night of PACAUT WOOD at 2.30 pm in the afternoon. 29 prisoners and two machine guns were captured and many casualties inflicted. Our casualties were slight. Twenty one machine guns co-operated, 11 being in the front line protecting the flanks of the raiders, very good work was done. 64,000 rounds being fired during the action which lasted 25 mins. Three guns were slightly damaged by shell fire. Except during the raid enemy artillery activity was normal. Our machine guns fired 10,000 rounds during the night carrying out the usual harassing fire.	Enc.
"	19/3/18		Enemy artillery was again very quiet during the day and many of our machine guns were out on the CANAL BANK and the FRONTLINE in the PACAUT SECTOR were intermittently shelled. A number of patrols were out on the Divisional front during the evening and night and many previously occupied posts and houses were found empty. Our machine guns fired 10,000 rounds during the night. Harassing various targets. An advance force has been made by the R.E. to clamp to the barrel casing for use in Pill boxes to carry away fumes. A preliminary test has been carried out and has proved satisfactory. Further tests are being arranged.	Enc.

WAR DIARY
or
INTELLIGENCE SUMMARY
(Erase heading not required.)

Army Form C. 2118.

Place	Date	Hour	Summary of Events and Information	Remarks and references to Appendices
In the field.	20/6/18		Enemy activity continued the greater at night than during the day. The CANAL BANK and tracks in the PACAUT SECTOR were harassed during the night. Enemy machine guns were also very active on tracks in our forward area. Fourteen balloons were up at one time during the day but enemy aircraft were inactive. Increased harassing fire is being carried out by our artillery and machine guns on all enemy forward position and enemy of communication.	Enr.
"	21/6/18		Another quiet day with increased activity at night. Much harassing fire was carried out by both sides. Our machine guns fired 34,000 rounds during the night on tracks and occupied dwellings. Enemy artillery were active on the Divisional front, harassing a suspected relief opposite the RIEZ, BERNENCHON and the CANAL BANK during the night. Enemy outpost line is very thinly held and our patrols have been very successful in obtaining prisoners for identification. Occupied shell holes have been surprised and the whole crews captured. They offer little or no resistance and three invariably been caught asleep. They state that during the night they work and during the day they sleep, no sentries being mounted.	Enr.

WAR DIARY
or
INTELLIGENCE SUMMARY.
(Erase heading not required.)

Army Form C. 2118.

Place	Date	Hour	Summary of Events and Information	Remarks and references to Appendices
Oulchy	22/7/18		During the day enemy activity was again below normal but increased harassing fire at night. Our machine guns were very active during the night, 29,000 rounds were fired on shellholes and tracks. During the evening our patrols were very active and much valuable information was gained. A day light patrol entered the enemy lines and surprised a post eight strong. No resistance was offered and the men were taken prisoners. Two tried to run away but these were shot by covering section.	Enn.
	23/7/18		Enemy artillery continues to be active during the night. LES HARISOIRS, Mt BERNENCHON, BLACKFRIARS BRIDGE, CANAL BANK and RIEZ DU VINAGE, being shelled at intervals. Our machine guns were also very active during the night.	Enn.
	24/7/18		As the result of the minor daylight operation 6 prisoners were captured. The usual method was adopted. The post was cautiously approached and then rushed, the Germans surrendering without offering any resistance. Enemy artillery was slightly more active during the day than previously, forward positions in the VINAGE SECTOR being shelled during the morning. Our trench artillery fire was carried out by our machine g	Enn.

WAR DIARY
or
INTELLIGENCE SUMMARY.

Army Form C. 2118.

Place	Date	Hour	Summary of Events and Information	Remarks and references to Appendices
Dickebush	25/7/18.		During the day enemy artillery activity was below normal. At midnight a portion the enemy front line opposite the VINAGE SECTOR was raided and found unoccupied. In reply the enemy put down a barrage on our front and support lines along the whole divisional front. Our machine guns fired 18,500 rounds in support this raid and also increased harassing fire was continued through the night.	Ean.
"	26/7/18		Normal harassing fire was carried out during the night by the enemy artillery after a very quiet day. A daylight patrol captured two men in an enemy post. Our machine guns carried out harassing fire on enemy communications during the night.	Ean.
"	27/7/18		Enemy artillery was slightly more active during the day than previously and normal at night. On our patrols a gun capture operations the occupants of an enemy post from HANTS FARM. During the night a stalwart man came out from HANTS FARM. During the night it was found that by firing in bursts below he was known if it would be liable clearing a entrance action. Bows wounded were found and it was found that by firing a slight pause the action could be carried on after firing ceased with considerable quantity that I gun then was found that a flight panic this cleared party. Corrected firing on the hill but had after a slight pause caused to harass enough away after the firing had ceased. No trace of the gunners could be found in the post hole.	Ean.

Army Form C. 2118.

WAR DIARY
or
INTELLIGENCE SUMMARY.
(Erase heading not required.)

Place	Date	Hour	Summary of Events and Information	Remarks and references to Appendices
In the Field	28/6		Enemy artillery was fairly active during the day and night. GONNEHEM, PACAUT WOOD, MT BERNENCHON, RIEZ DU VINAGE, BELLERIVE and NOSECAP ROAD being intermittently shelled. GONNEHEM receiving particular attention throughout the period. His patrol left our lines and brought back important information regarding enemy work on front line posts. Our guns engaged targets during the night and 700 rounds fired. Our planes were very active. 2 E.A. were forced to land behind their own lines and one Observation balloon was brought down.	Ecu
	29/6		A day light patrol enquired an enemy post shell consisting of 7 NCO and 4 men and captured them. Enemy activity during the period was normal. He moved harassing fire being carried out. Our machine gun fired 12,500 during the night harassing enemy forward communication and occupied shell holes.	Ecu
	30/6		Two more prisoners captured by one of our patrols. They approved a post which showed some resistance the NCO in charge (a Sergt Maj.) was killed and another private surrendered. Enemy artillery engaged narrow targets during the period. Our machine gun carried out the usual harassing fire.	Ecu

Army Form C. 2118.

WAR DIARY
or
INTELLIGENCE SUMMARY
(Erase heading not required.)

Instructions regarding War Diaries and Intelligence Summaries are contained in F.S. Regs., Part II. and the Staff Manual respectively. Title pages will be prepared in manuscript.

Place	Date	Hour	Summary of Events and Information	Remarks and references to Appendices
Suck field	3/7/18		There was a considerable increase in enemy artillery harassing fire during the night. MT BERNENCHON, LES HARISOIRS. NORTH R.B. and the TAK at BANK being intermittently shelled throughout the night. Our guns fired 10,000 rounds harassing fire on tracks and occupied shellholes during the night.	Cav.

Original

4 Bn M.G Corps

Army Form C. 2118.

WAR DIARY
or
INTELLIGENCE SUMMARY.
(Erase heading not required.)

Instructions regarding War Diaries and Intelligence Summaries are contained in F. S. Regs., Part II. and the Staff Manual respectively. Title pages will be prepared in manuscript.

Place	Date	Hour	Summary of Events and Information	Remarks and references to Appendices
In the field	1/8/18		There was a slight increase in harassing fire by enemy artillery during the night. LES HARISOIRS, CANAL BANK and MT BERNENCHON and NOSECAP ROAD were shelled intermittently. Our machine guns fired 9000 rounds during the night on enemy posts and tracks.	Enc.
"	2/8/18		Considerable increase in enemy artillery activity both day and night. Scattered shelling of whole forward area was experienced out and during the morning 30 rounds of 21cm were fired into BUSNETTES and CENSE LAVALLEE. Our patrols were very active and one and many enemy forward posts were found unoccupied. During the night our machine guns in conjunction with the field artillery harassed selected occupied areas. 20,000 rounds were fired during the day & following night by R.A and M.G fire. E.A. were very active and there were numerous O/F by R.A and M.G fire. E.A. flew over our lines.	Enc.
"	3/8/18		At 9.30 a.m an enemy barrage was put down on BUTTER SUPPORT — the VINAGE SECTION and about two Platoons were observed collecting behind DESERTED FARM. On rifle and Lewis Gun fire being opened, Barrelino undoubtedly a raid was contemplated but it was frustrated by the above own action. Artillery activity during the remainder of the day & evening was nothing unusual. Our machine Guns fired 21,000 rounds harassing light the nightline normal. in conjunction with the Artillery.	Enc.

Original

WAR DIARY
INTELLIGENCE SUMMARY
(Erase heading not required.)

Army Form C. 2118.

Place	Date	Hour	Summary of Events and Information	Remarks and references to Appendices
In the field	4/9/18		During the day our Infantry patrols pushed forward in the PACAUT SECTION and occupied the old German front line which was found unoccupied. It is reported that the enemy are entrenching and close touch is being maintained by our Infantry. Enemy artillery activity normal - the usual harassing fire being carried on during the night. Our machine guns fired at our normal rate in conjunction with the field artillery engaging selected targets during the night.	Cav.
	5/9/18		Patrols continued to push forward and our line along the whole Divisional front has been advanced thousand yards. They are in touch with the enemy and forward posts are being established. Our machine guns did not fire during the night owing to the uncertainty of the location of our advanced patrols. Enemy artillery was quiet during the day but very active at night on our forward area.	Cav.
	6/9/18		Our patrols have now pushed forward to a depth of 2000 yards to commence of position was encountered from the ridge of QUENTIN. Snipers and MG posts are holding the houses. These are pushed and the village occupied. The old main line of resistance is to be held perfect our machine gun positions with the exception of 9/18 guns from (4 S.A. Coy and H 9/18 Coy.)	Cav.

WAR DIARY or INTELLIGENCE SUMMARY

Army Form C. 2118.

Place	Date	Hour	Summary of Events and Information	Remarks and references to Appendices
Wh. Huts.	6/6/18 (Cont).		Each Brigade has pushed forward an outpost Battalion and these Bn. have four machine guns attached to them.	
"	7/18		During the night our patrols pushed forward and occupied the line of the TURBEAUTE stream. On the right they were held up by occupied houses in the village of PACAUT. The enemy appear to be holding this line very strongly, as all attempts of our patrols to continue the advance met with stern opposition. Fortunately the weather continues to be warm and dry otherwise the ground would be almost untenable. During wet weather this district is practically a bog and everywhere the ground is marshy. Enemy Artillery continues to be very active day and night and main attention being paid to our old front line PACAUT WOOD, CORNETMALO, PIERRE AU BEURE and RIEZ-DU-VINAGE were also heavily shelled.	Fine.
"	8/18		Along the whole Divisional front enemy activity continues to be extremely active day and night. The new forward area and our old front and support lines were heavily shelled and our old established E. of the TURBEAUTE LINE but these were driven in by a strong enemy counter-attack. With the exception of this the Germans attacked but no infantry infantry all posts in now established no movement to carried out during the night.	Fine.

WAR DIARY
or
INTELLIGENCE SUMMARY.

Army Form C. 2118.

Place	Date	Hour	Summary of Events and Information	Remarks and references to Appendices
In the field	9/5/18		Marked decrease in hostile shelling activity during the day. At night harassing fire was carried out on front and support lines PACAUT SECTION; PACAUT WOOD CANAL BANK and RIEZ du VINAGE. The enemy's resistance to the advance of our patrols has considerably stiffened apparent that he have dug themselves in on the line of the TAU BEAUTE Eau STREAM. An observation balloon was brought down in flames at 10.30 opposite the divisional front by our planes.	Eau.
"	10/5/18		Enemy artillery was very active during the morning over our forward area particularly in the vicinity of QUENTIN, RIEZ du VINAGE, PIERRE-AU-BEURE, PACAUT WOOD and the CANAL BANK also received some attention. During the night E A were very active. Bombs were dropped on back area, and on the CANAL BANK and LES HARISOIRS. Work on pill boxes and emplacements in our main line of defence continues on this line is being maintained.	Eau.
"	11/5/18		The situation is becoming more normal and activity on both sides is decreasing. During the day it was fairly quiet and normal harassing fire was carried out during the night. Our machine gun fire has not yet been moved forward so that no harassing can be carried out.	Eau.

WAR DIARY
or
INTELLIGENCE SUMMARY.

Army Form C. 2118.

(Erase heading not required.)

Place	Date	Hour	Summary of Events and Information	Remarks and references to Appendices
In the field	12/5/18		Taylor. Quiet day & night. Enemy artillery harassed LES HARRISOIRS during the night. A H.V. long range gun fired 20 rounds into the area round Bn. headquarters at BEUVRIES during the day. The crops which have long been a source of trouble are now being harvested by experienced farmers drawn from the Infantry. French civilians have also been allowed to assist, to collect their own crop.	Enc.
"	13/5/18		Hostile artillery increased enemy trajectory. PACAUTWOOD and CANAL BANK and RIEZ DU VINAGE were heavily shelled at intervals. Our patrols were very active and a number of enemy posts were located. Enemy aircraft were fairly active during the day and night, fine bombs being dropped in the vicinity of the Canal Bank.	Enc.
"	14/5/18		Our forward guns are assisting with harassing fire on the outpost line and now rolled down 1500 rounds were fired on enemy communication. Hostile artillery was fairly quiet during the whole period, as the result of our artillery fire, were observed behind the enemy line. During the night numerous flares, & Enemy aircraft continue the very active at night, bombs been dropped on back areas.	Enc.

WAR DIARY
INTELLIGENCE SUMMARY

Army Form C. 2118.

Original

Place	Date	Hour	Summary of Events and Information	Remarks and references to Appendices
In the field	16/9/18		Enemy shelling slightly above normal during day. LES HARISOIRS & area between old front & support line receiving special attention. During the night PACAUT WOOD & CANAL BANK shelled with H.E. & gas. Our forward guns fired 2000 Rds on important road junctions, houses & occupied shell holes. Enemy bombing planes again active during night.	H.J.
"	16/9/18		Our Machine Guns active during night harassing Rds & tracks. Hostile artillery less active than usual. 5" Enemy En's flying planes were seen over our lines during the day. One of our machines was brought down in enemy lines by A.A. fire.	H.J.
"	17/9/18		Infantry patrols established a new post at Q.35.b.4.6. otherwise no change in our line of posts. Hostile artillery fire normal. CANAL BANK & PACAUT WOOD receiving are attention with 10.5cm & 15cm. Our machine guns fired 8000 Rds on selected targets during the night. Enemy dirigible balloon brought down in flames by one of our planes. Several explosions were heard in vicinity of PARADIS & during afternoon numerous fires were seen in LAVENTIE.	H.J.

WAR DIARY
or
INTELLIGENCE SUMMARY.

Army Form C. 2118.

Place	Date	Hour	Summary of Events and Information	Remarks and references to Appendices
In the field	18/8/18		There are signs indicating that a further retirement on the part of the enemy is contemplated opposite our front. Our Infantry patrols were again very active & pushed forward EAST of PARADIS ROAD. Hostile artillery normal.	J.W.
	19/8/18		CANAL BANK, BUTTER FARM & HUN FARM shelled slightly during night. Machine guns fired on important road junctions. Hun aero-planes were very active. Diacken in recruits. One hostile enemy plane was brought down by Lewis gun fire during the afternoon. Infantry patrols again pushed forward & established forward posts. Enemy artillery considerably below normal activity. Enemy indication that guns are being taken further back.	J.W.
	20/8/18		Our 2 forward machine guns moved 400 yds forward & took up suitable positions, no firing was done however owing to uncertainty of exact location of advanced patrols. Enemy artillery quiet by day & night in this section. E.A. active during night bombing back areas.	J.W.

Army Form C. 2118.

WAR DIARY
or
INTELLIGENCE SUMMARY.
(Erase heading not required.)

Original

Instructions regarding War Diaries and Intelligence
Summaries are contained in F. S. Regs., Part II.
and the Staff Manual respectively. Title pages
will be prepared in manuscript.

Place	Date	Hour	Summary of Events and Information	Remarks and references to Appendices
In the field	21/9/18		Hostile artillery still very quiet. Few gas shells nr HATE FARM & small shells dropped at intervals during night in HINGES RIDGE. 1 E.A. only seen during day flying very high & in direction of BUSNES. Enemy balloon brought down in flames opposite right sector.	JNL
	22/9/18		Intermittent shelling of CANAL JANE, HINGES & RIEZ during night otherwise quiet. A considerable number of yellow lights & flares were sent up opposite divisional front followed by slight shelling & M.G. fire. Hostile M.G.s more active than usual, apparently firing at our patrols pushing forward. Enemy observation balloons seem to have been moved back a considerable distance during past 2 days.	JNL
	23/9/18		The 4th & 14th Divisions today will be relieved & relieved this Division. This Battn on relief assembles at LE VALLÉ and LECLERC preparatory to being transferred to First Army.	JNL

Army Form C. 2118.

WAR DIARY
or
INTELLIGENCE SUMMARY.

(Erase heading not required.)

Instructions regarding War Diaries and Intelligence Summaries are contained in F. S. Regs., Part II. and the Staff Manual respectively. Title pages will be prepared in manuscript.

Places	Date	Hour	Summary of Events and Information	Remarks and references to Appendices
In the field	24/8/18		The Division was today transferred to the First Army (XXII Corps). The Battn entrained at BURNETTES 8.30 AM & was conveyed to BAILLEUL-LES-PERNES where it rested for the night	JWL
	25/8/18		The Battn marched from BAILLEUL-LES-PERNES to VILLERS & then entrained for BRYAS, from BRYAS the Battn marched to ROELLECOURT & rested for the night being billeted in villages & vicinity	JWL
	26/8/18		Battalion again moved forward, marching to AUBIGNY where it was billeted preparatory to moving for transport to the Canadian Corps.	JWL
	27/8/18		The Battalion rested for the day at AUBIGNY.	JWL
	28/8/18		The 4th Division has now been transferred to the Canadian Corps & preparatory to relieving the 3rd Canadian Division moves to front F of ARRAS.	JWL

WAR DIARY
or
INTELLIGENCE SUMMARY

Army Form C. 2118.

Original   Secret

Place	Date	Hour	Summary of Events and Information	Remarks and references to Appendices
In the field	28/4		For the purpose of the relieve the Batt⁰ was attacked as under.	
			"A" Company to 11th Inf. Brigade	
			"B" " " 12 " "	
			"C" " " 10 " "	
			"D" " " in reserve.	
			The whole entrained & were taken to a point West of ARRAS. It being found impossible to take lorries any further forward owing to enemy shelling ARRAS - CAMBRAI Rd. During the day the Brigades & this Batt⁰ relieved 3rd Canadian Division.	Nil.
	29/4		Considerable enemy artillery activity. ARRAS - CAMBRAI Rd was a constant target. Areas on both sides of road reached with HE & shrapnel MONCHY heavily shelled at intervals throughout day. 12 hostile flying enemy planes were over Bn front from 11.30 to 12 noon, & several small squadrons attempted to cross our lines but were driven off by AA fire. About 11 AM 2 E.A. were driven down by our aircraft. All our machine guns are now in position & A, B & C Company	Nil.

WAR DIARY
or
INTELLIGENCE SUMMARY

Army Form C. 2118.

August

Place	Date	Hour	Summary of Events and Information	Remarks and references to Appendices
In the field	30/8/18		Hostile artillery very active throughout day & night. Line of SENSÉE RIVER heavily shelled. ETERPIGNY WOOD, BOIS BOUFFLARD & LONGWOOD shelled from 5.30 to 7 AM. The infantry successfully advanced our line E of GREENLAND HILL & captured PLOUVAIN. The village of ETERPIGNY has also been captured. Aircraft on both sides exceptionally active. Bombs were dropped from enemy planes in vicinity of MONCHY.	N.Y.R.
	31/8/18		Usual harassing fire carried out by hostile artillery excl. distinct receiving attention during day & night. CAMBRAI R.D. & VIS-EN-ARTOIS shelled heavily but our artillery were very active during night harassing & also firing hours of S.O.S. signal. Hostile flying enemy planes over our lines Nil. at intervals. Our machine guns swept forward in order to enforce our infantry who have advanced successfully. Kept 2 bys. Enemy M. Gs. have been exceptionally active during	N.Y.R.

Past 24 hours

To:- 4th. Division

46/6561

Herewith Original of War
Diary for month of September.

5/10/18.   Eawilliam Capt &adjt.
          for Lt. Col.,
          Comdg. 4th. Battn. MGC

Army Form C. 2118.

WAR DIARY
or
INTELLIGENCE SUMMARY.
(Erase heading not required.)

Places	Date	Hour	Summary of Events and Information	Remarks and references to Appendices
In the field.	1/9/18		Naval harassing fire by both artillery. East district getting a lien during day & night. BOIS de SOUTHARD shelled continuously throughout 24 hrs; also ETERPIGNY REMY WOOD RIDGE also shells. Enemy aircraft active throughout day. Planes over BOIS de SART at 3 P.M. & 7 P.M. driven off by M.G. fire. M.Gs guns & searchlight to Brigade covered forward with the absence of Infantry.	Hel.
	2/9/18		In co-operation with the Canadian Corps the 4th (British) Div. attacked enemy positions. The new objective being the DROCOURT - QUEANT line. 24 Guns under Major Sheriff of "D" Coy. took up a position between the junction of the SENSEE & COSEUL Rivers & point P.8.C.0.6. 8 guns move forward to protect flank & remaining 16 in 2 groups of 8 each fired the Barrage in the village of ETAING. The 11th Div. machine guns to operate in these but other guns remained with Brigade & carried out rôle given by Brigade commanders will complete success. All objectives were attained by Div. & enemy pushed back before he...	See

Army Form C. 2118.

WAR DIARY
of
INTELLIGENCE SUMMARY.
(Erase heading not required.)

Instructions regarding War Diaries and Intelligence Summaries are contained in F.S. Regs., Part II. and the Staff Manual respectively. Title pages will be prepared in manuscript.

Place	Date	Hour	Summary of Events and Information	Remarks and references to Appendices
In the Field	3/9/18		after complete success of operations & reorganisation of line Bns were given orders for relief. This took place during the afternoon by the 1st Divn & the 14th Divn were bivouacs for night. Battalion old positions before the advance. The 1st guns tents Major Shoff marche at GRANGE HUT with "D" Coy. The remaining 6 guns teams etc of Battr were ordered to meet at CROSS RDS. TOLLOY-LES-MOFFLINES ready to embus by 2PM 4th inst.	Att.
	4/9/18		The Battn entrained at TOLLOY-LES-MOFFLINES crossrds with 12th Bde Group at 3.P.M. & detrained at TINQUES 6.30.P.M. The transport left ARRAS at 12 Noon reaching MONCHY BRETON at 5.P.M. after debussing the Battn formed up & marched to MONCHY BRETON, the village allotted for billets.	Att.
	5/9/18		" "	Att.
	6/9/18		Battalion in training at Monchy BRETON.	Att.

Army Form C. 2118.

WAR DIARY
or
INTELLIGENCE SUMMARY.
(Erase heading not required.)

Place	Date	Hour	Summary of Events and Information	Remarks and references to Appendices
In the Field	7 9/18		Battalion in training at MONCHY BRETON	Nil
	8 9/18		" " " "	Nil
	9 9/18		" " " "	Nil
	10 9/18		" " " "	Nil
	11 9/18		" " " "	Nil
	12 9/18		" " " "	Nil
	13 9/18		" " " "	Nil
	14 9/18		" " " "	Nil
	15 9/18		" " " "	Nil
	16 9/18		" " " "	Nil
	17 9/18		D Coy attached to the 16th Inf. Bde. embarked at TINQUES for ST ROHART'S FACTORY on the CAMBRAI Rd. and relieved the LEFT Brigade of the 56th Division. Eight gun position were taken over from Brigade & Company HQ.	Recon
	18 9/18		on the night 18/19th and 6 men kept in reserve at Company HQ. The Division is taking over the defensive flank along the River SCARPE, River TRINQUIS and SENSÉE River	

WAR DIARY or INTELLIGENCE SUMMARY

Place	Date	Hour	Summary of Events and Information	Remarks and references to Appendices
In the Field	16/9/18 cont		with the 10th Bn holding the Right Section on L'ÉCLUSE SECTION.	Sear
"	19/18		A and B Companies embussed at MINGOVAL with the 11th Infantry Bde. and advanced on the FEUCHY CHAPEL ROAD and relieved the 8/11th Divisions on the HAMBLAIN SECTION along the River Scarpe. On the night of the 19/20th 6 guns of D Coy completed the relief taking over 6 positions of B Coy 56th Bn in the L'ÉCLUSE Section. The enemy had denied the enemy so that the whole of the area immediately in front of the Divisional outpost line is flooded and only a few causeways exist affording crossings on the inundated country. The Division are holding a 12,000' frontage and the machine gun are scattered over the whole area. Great difficulty has been experienced in maintaining communications and control of the Bn. To alleviate this Maj. SHARPE O.C. B Coy has been Group Commander of A and B Coys with a Head Quarters at 11th Bde. Many difficulties have been experienced owing to relief on account of Companies being attached to Brigades and reverting to the Command of the O.C. M.G. Bn. on completion.	

WAR DIARY or INTELLIGENCE SUMMARY

Army Form C. 2118.

Place	Date	Hour	Summary of Events and Information	Remarks and references to Appendices
Outpts	Feb 20/18		Bn. HQ and 'C' Company entrained at MONCHY BRETON for ANNEZIN BLANGY ANNEZ. 'C' Coy is the reserve company and billets in it. BLANGY ANNEZ, Bn. HQ being situated with Divisional HQ at Place St Croix ARRAS. The M.G. Companies attached to this Bde (LINCOLNSHIRE and EAST RIDING YEO) M.G.C. come under the command of the O.C. M.G. Bn. and are distributed as follows:- A and B Coys 4 Bn M.G.C. and A Coy 102 Bn in the HAMBLAIN Section under Group Commander Maj Sherrill. D Coy 4 Bn M.G.C. in the L'ECLUSE Section under Maj Sharpe. C Coy 4 Bn M.G.C. in the BLANGY and B Coy 102 Bn in ORANGE HILL Area in reserve. In the line infantry patrols were busy examining the enemy's wire across the flooded area and the extent of the floods. Enemy artillery activity was confined to harassing fire. Our machine guns were inactive.	Erase

WAR DIARY
or
INTELLIGENCE SUMMARY.

Army Form C. 2118.

Place	Date	Hour	Summary of Events and Information	Remarks and references to Appendices
Whitfield	21/9/18		Artillery activity was normal, being confined to intermittent shelling of roads and woods in the divisional area. Fairly quiet during the day, although enemy machine guns showed some activity and own were inactive.	Ew.
"	22/9/18		Our patrols have been very active, also German dumps of material for bridging were discovered and places suitable for crossing the river TRINQUIS reconnoitred. The roads in the HAMBLAIN sector reported ploughed & planted. Enemy activity normal – Artillery showing communications intermittently throughout the period.	Ew.
"	23/9/18		Very quiet day. Enemy artillery and aircraft activity below normal. "B" Coy 102nd Bn relieved "B" Coy 4th Bn in the HAMBLAIN sector during the night 23/9/nt. "B" Coy 4th BnC.C. moved into Pueblo in MOMAY area – the orange hill area being evacuated.	Ew.
"	24/9/18		Early this morning the enemy raided Hoo & Orpington posts and obtained identification owing to our pickets and the post was a Lewis gun from our post. Him to be evacuated leaving three wounded men. Another quiet day. Enemy artillery being abnormally quiet though our artillery.	Ew.

Army Form C. 2118.

WAR DIARY
or
INTELLIGENCE SUMMARY.
(Erase heading not required.)

Instructions regarding War Diaries and Intelligence Summaries are contained in F. S. Regs., Part II. and the Staff Manual respectively. Title pages will be prepared in manuscript.

Place	Date	Hour	Summary of Events and Information	Remarks and references to Appendices
In the field.	26/9/18		Outposts were very active during the night reconnoitring posts across the marshes and flooded area. Very valuable information was obtained, and casualties inflicted on enemy patrols encountered. Incessant hostile artillery activity especially during the night. GALLEY WOOD, BOIRY LANE, VICTORIA COPSE and the vicinity of Bn Right Bn H.Q. being pelted with Yellow Cross Gas shells. Many fires have been recently observed at night, behind the enemy line.	Encs
"	26/9/18		Enemy artillery action normal. During the night our Infantry attempted a foot patrol but the current proved too strong for them to cross the Tournepire River. During the day ETAING, BOIRY, N. of ETERPIGNY and GALLEY WOOD were shelled. Machine Guns on both sides were inactive.	Encs 1
"	27/9/18		At 5.35am an attack was launched towards CAMBRAI. B and C Companies were attached to 56th Bn and formed No.1 Group and they Maj. Styles. These guns were engaged in harassing fire and did very good work. There were no casualties and Guns were slightly damaged by splinters.	Encs

Army Form C. 2118.

WAR DIARY
or
INTELLIGENCE SUMMARY.
(Erase heading not required.)

Place	Date	Hour	Summary of Events and Information	Remarks and references to Appendices
In trenches	27/9/18 cont		At the same time the Divisions on the 51st Division put up a Chinese attack with our M/R SCARPE. Dummy figures were erected and attracted considerable hostile fire. A Coy assisted with 4 guns and fired Boro-da. The enemy reply to our barrage was negligible. The guns attacked kite & & Ben fired 250,000 rounds in support of the operations which were entirely successful.	Cow.
"	28 "	9h	Hostile activity below normal. As the result of minor operations bridge heads have been established across the FLOQUET area in the L'ECLUSE. 2,500 rds were fired by our M.Gs in support of these operations during Quiet day with increased activity at night. 15/A dropped 12 bombs on our back areas in the vicinity of Re COURT WOOD and TE BOIS DU SART.	Cow.
"	29 "	9h	During the night a bridge was constructed across the TRINQUIS river and 3 posts established. Throughout the flooded area continued to drop as we have & flown up the Chemise Gate. Our artillery had a shoot in the afternoon which continued till dawn and also enemy activity generally has been normal increasing during the night.	Cow.

D. D. & L., London, E.C.
(A8001) Wt. W.1774/M291 5/17 750,000 Sch. 52 Forms/C2118/4

WAR DIARY
or
INTELLIGENCE SUMMARY

Army Form C. 2118.

Place	Date	Hour	Summary of Events and Information	Remarks and references to Appendices
In the field	30/9/18		Marked increase in hostile activity during the day. DURY, ETAING, ETERPIGNY and QUARRY at Q.13.c.1.9 and CAMBRAI Rd being frequently shelled. Enemy artillery were also active on the HAMBLAIN Sector. The 10th Bde extended their flank to the night taking in the 56 Bn. This village was captured with resistance active operations on the 29th. Village of PALLUEL from the 56 Bn. "C" Coy of 44th Bn M.G. relieved "B" Coy 58th Bn in train and "C" and "D" Coys of 4th Bn M.G. were formed into one group with Maj. W.R. Stipho in Command.	Corres

SECRET

To:- 4th Division

> 4TH BATTALION
> MACHINE GUN
> CORPS.
>
> No. 1/33
> Date................

   Herewith War Diary for month of
October.

                              T.H. Darwell Major
                          for Lt. Colonel,
7/11/18   Commdg. 4th. Battn. Machine Gun Corps.

W.C.9

CONFIDENTIAL

WAR DIARY

OF

4TH BATTALION. MACHINE GUN CORPS

FROM 1st October 1918 To 31st October 1918.

Army Form C. 2118.

WAR DIARY
or
INTELLIGENCE SUMMARY.
(Erase heading not required.)

Instructions regarding War Diaries and Intelligence
Summaries are contained in F. S. Regs., Part II.
and the Staff Manual respectively. Title pages
will be prepared in manuscript.

Place	Date	Hour	Summary of Events and Information	Remarks and references to Appendices
In the Field	1/10/18		Fairly Quiet day with increased aerial activity during the night. Various considerable aerial activity during the night. Bombs were dropped on GUEMAPPE, ÉCOURT ST QUENTIN and RECOURT. During the day considerable movement was observed behind the enemy lines and a large number of fires in towns and villages were seen.	Eaw.
	2/10/18		Increased activity during the day especially near Boiry, and during the night BOIRY was subjected to a slight gas bombardment. Considerable movement and a large number of fires were again observed. Harassing fire was carried out by our machine gun posts across the TRINQUIS BROOK, but no attempt was made by the enemy to counter them. Enemy withdrawal has not commenced although there are indications of preparation for withdrawal.	Eaw.
	3/10/18		Hostile artillery again very active. Our patrols established	Eaw.
	4/10/18		Harassing fire was carried out during the night on enemy communications by the machine gun. Hostile activity was below normal although enemy infantry made three attempts to raid our advanced posts. These were driven off by rifle & machine gun fire.	Eaw.

Army Form C. 2118.

WAR DIARY
or
INTELLIGENCE SUMMARY.
(Erase heading not required.)

Instructions regarding War Diaries and Intelligence Summaries are contained in F.S. Regs., Part II. and the Staff Manual respectively. Title pages will be prepared in manuscript.

Place	Date	Hour	Summary of Events and Information	Remarks and references to Appendices
In the field	5/10/16		The enemy again attacked our forward posts and one M.G. firer in reply to the S.O.S. Hostile artillery was active on forward posts. Considerable fire were again observed behind the enemy lines.	Ears.
	6/10/16		Enemy activity was normal. The Division is being relieved in the line by the 1st Canadian Division. The machine guns are to be relieved on the night 7th/8th as soon after the infantry.	Ears.
	7/10/16		The Infantry relief was quite successful. The 8th Bn on our left carried out a minor operation at dawn and took the village of BIACHE ST VAAST. Some of the guns of A Coy assisted in the operation by enfilading the FRESNES - ROUVROY line. Bn H.Q. moved to WARLUS.	Ears.
	8/10/16		The machine gun relief was quite successful. The companies marched during the night to railway. A and B Coy arriving at 4.30 a.m. and C and D Coys staying the night at MONCHY, arriving at 12 midday.	Ears.

WAR DIARY
or
INTELLIGENCE SUMMARY.
(Erase heading not required.)

Army Form C. 2118.

Place	Date	Hour	Summary of Events and Information	Remarks and references to Appendices
In the field	9/7/18		B Coy 10th took part in a practice operation with the 15th Inf. Bde. the other companies overhauled guns and equipment and generally cleaning up.	Eau.
"	10/7/18		Batts. arranged for toutes Bn. Orders received to proceed tomorrow.	Eau.
	11/7/18		Lt. Col. Vennica D.S.O. resume command of the Bn. Lt. Col. Ott North D.S.O. has gone to England on a course. Bn moved to RAILLENCOURT by bus. Transport moved by road staying the night at WANCOURT.	Eau.
	12/7/18		Bn moved to ST OLLES.	Eau.
	13/7/18		Battalion moved to ESCAUDOEUVRE.	Eau.
"	14/7/18		Battalion training	Eau.
"	15/7/18		"	Eau.
	16/7/18		"	Eau.
	17/7/18		Reconnoitred front line. Orders received to relieve 4th Division in the trenches.	Eau.

WAR DIARY
INTELLIGENCE SUMMARY

Place	Date	Hour	Summary of Events and Information	Remarks and references to Appendices
LKfwd	18/10		D Coy relieved the right Company of the 245th Bn.	Errs.
"	19/10		A, B and C Coys. moved into the line, and Bn HQ moved to Thiant. Preparations were made for an attack on the morning 9/20th. C Coy on our right with 10th Inf Bde. and A Coy with 11th Inf Bde. Information received that the enemy was retiring and that the 10th Inf Bde. patrols were through the village of SAULZOIR and established on their first line. On the left the enemy continued shoot posts in the village of HASPRES.	Errs.
"	20/10		At 0200 the morning of the 10th Bde. tn th Bde. attacked and secured the final objective. The village of HASPRES is in our hands and our infantry are established on the final objective. A and C Coys have moved forward and taken up positions on the exercise Territory. The Right Brigade moved forward in the direction of VERCHAIN very little opposition being met with.	Errs.
"	21/10		The day was spent consolidating our gains, and the infantry are in close touch with the enemy. Hostile Artillery has been fairly active. An advanced Bn HQ was established near Villerrover CAUCHIE.	Errs.

WAR DIARY
or
INTELLIGENCE SUMMARY
(Erase heading not required.)

Army Form C. 2118.

Place	Date	Hour	Summary of Events and Information	Remarks and references to Appendices
Wakefield	22/10		Infantry patrols upon the villages of MONCHAUX and VERCHAIN. Clear of the enemy and are in touch with his rear guards. Preparations are made for an attack on the morning of the 23rd. But not to capture QUERENAING.	Erw.
"	23/10		Bn HQ moved to AVESNES-LE-SEC advanced Bn HQ being withdrawn. The enemy still hold the ground between the villages of MONCHAUX and VERCHAIN.	Erw.
"	24/10		At 0400 hrs the morning the Div attacked and captured the villages of MONCHAUX and VERCHAIN and the high ground to the east. Very little resistance was met with because the enemy surrendered freely. D Coy moved forward in close support to the 16th Inf Bde on the night and B Coy in close support to 11th Inf Bde on the left. A and C Coys assisted the attack by placing down a barrage. The operation was entirely successful and good work was done by the machine guns in support.	Erw. 0400 Wakefield Saw

WAR DIARY
or
INTELLIGENCE SUMMARY.
(Erase heading not required.)

Army Form C. 2118.

Place	Date	Hour	Summary of Events and Information	Remarks and references to Appendices
Inkfield	25/10/18		During the night 24/25th Oct. the Riverand front was taken over by the 12th Infantry Bde. who exploited yesterday's success. C Coy were ordered to on close support to assist in any success obtained. The villages of QUERENAING and ARTRES were taken. It was found impossible the high ground to the east. It was found impossible to hold the high ground and our troops retired alarming bridge heads across the river RHONELLE near ARTRES. A Coy was sent up in support to maintain that bridge head.	Ean.
Inkfields	26/10/18		Bn advanced HQ established at VERCHAIN. Dispositions of the Bn are at present: C Coy in line with 12th Inf Bde. A Coy in close support. B Coy in reserve and D Coy in Billets at VERCHAIN.	Ean.
"	27/10	10	Dispositions unchanged, and bridgeheads across the RHONELLE river maintained. B Coy altered to HASPRES to Billets	Ean.

Army Form C. 2118.

WAR DIARY
or
INTELLIGENCE SUMMARY
(Erase heading not required.)

Place	Date	Hour	Summary of Events and Information	Remarks and references to Appendices
In K/field.	28/10/18		Preparations are being made to continue the attack on a future date to capture the village of PRESEAU and the high ground to the East S.E.	0010 battalion Ears.
"	29/10/18		Hostile artillery fairly active other wise nothing to report. attack postpones to the 31st.	Ears.
"	30/18 to 31/18		attack postponed to 1st/11/18.	Ears. Ears.

1/10/18	1 O.R. Killed in action 1 O.R. reinforcement	13/10/18	2 O.Rs. Reinforcements 2 O.Rs. Hospital
2/10/18	26 O.Rs. Reinforcements 1 O.R. hospital	14/10/18	3 O.Rs. Reinforcements
3/10/18	1 O.R. hospital Lieut. E.H. ROSE to U.K. for course	15/10/18	Lieuts COMERY & MANNING to U.K. substitution 2/Lieut. T.C.W. INSKIP to U.K. for transfer to R.A.F.
4/10/18	4 O.Rs. Hospital	16/10/18	17 O.Rs. reinforcements
5/10/18	3 O.Rs. reinforcements 1 O.R. hospital	17/10/18	2 O.Rs. wounded
6/10/18	1 O.R. reinforcement 1 O.R. hospital Lt. Col. O.H. NORTH to U.K.	18/10/18	2 O.Rs wounded (at duty) 4 O.Rs. hospital
7/10/18	1 O.R. hospital	19/10/18	1 O.R. Killed in action 5 O.R. wounded Lieut. PRATT.T. and 3 O.Rs. hospital
8/10/18	Lt. Col. W.A.T.B. SOMERVILLE D.S.O joined for command	20/10/18	1 O.R. acc. Injured 1 O.R. wounded (at duty)
9/10/18	2/Lieut. J.S. CLAPHAM joined 4 O.Rs. hospital	21/10/18	7 O.Rs. hospital
10/10/18	Lieut. ALLEN.H.G. M.C. to hospital Lieut. HAWKINS.E.J. to hospital 7 O.Rs. hospital Lieut. H.G. ALLEN M.C. rejoined	22/10/18	1 O.R. wounded 1 O.R. acc. injured
11/10/18	-- NIL --	23/10/18	7 O.Rs. hospital
12/10/18	-- NIL --	24/10/18	Lieut. E.R. STEVEN wounded 6 O.Rs. wounded Capt. J.L. HARPER and 2 O.Rs hospital

25/10/18	Lieut.L.V.H.GINGELL 2/Lieut.A.D.GOWANS " G.C.GARNETT and 11 O.R.s reinforcements	29/10/18	9 O.Rs. Hospital 2 O.Rs.reinforcements 2 O.Rs.wounded
26/10/18	5 O.Rs.to hospital 2 O.Rs. wounded 2/Lieut.E.A.BOYCE wounded	30/10/18	1 O.R. reinforcement 2 O.Rs.wounded 1 O.R.gassed 2/Lieut.C.A.KNEE wounded
27/10/18	2/Lieut.J.S.CLAPHAM and 3 O.Rs.hospital Major R.D.HODGSON wounded 3 O.Rs.wounded 1 O.R. killed in action	31/10/18	5 O.Rs.hospital 2 O.Rs.wounded
28/10/18	3 O.Rs hospital 4 O.Rs. Reinf.		

SECRET   COPY NO. 13

4th. BATTALION MACHINE GUN CORPS INSTRUCTIONS FOR OFFENCE NO.2

Map Ref. 51A N.E. and S.E. 1/20000   October 23rd. 1918.

1   GENERAL PLAN

    On the 24th.October 1918 the 4th. Division will attack and
    capture the villages of VERCHAIN and MONCHAUX and high ground
    to the East.
    The 10th. Infantry Brigade will attack on the right; the 11th.
    Infantry Brigade on the Left.
    On night 24/25th. October the Divisional Front will be taken
    over by the 12th. Infantry Brigade.

2   BOUNDARIES AND OBJECTIVES

    The Divisional and Brigade boundaries and objectives have been issued to all
    concerned.

3   DETAILS OF ACTION OF 4th. BATTALION MACHINE GUN CORPS

    (a) "C" Company from positions in P.23.a. will place a barrage on
        QUARRIES in P.12.b. and on SUNKEN ROADS running N.E. from
        P.6.c.5.0.
        Time:- Zero to Zero plus 30
        At Zero plus 60 all guns will lift from their targets to MUR
        COPSE where barrage will remain until Zero plus 80
        At Zero plus 80 fire will cease.
        Rate of fire:- One belt in five minutes
        At Zero plus 80 the   Company will move to positions in
        P.17.c. and P.16.b. from which guns can cover slopes in P.6.
        in case of counter-attack breaking through in this Area.

    (b) "A" Company from positions in P.10.c. will place a barrage on
        SUNKEN ROAD running North from P.6.c.1.0. and on SUNKEN ROAD
        running N.E. from P.5.d.2.6.
        Time:- Zero to Zero plus 60
        Rate of fire:- 1 belt in 5 minutes
        At Zero plus 60 the Company will take up positions in P.10 and
        P.3. from which guns can cover slopes East of BLUE LINE in
        P.5.a. and b. and P.34.d. in case of counter-attack
        breaking through in this Area.

    (c) "D" Company will assemble in P.21 (guns and belt boxes on
        limbers) and will move forward at Zero plus 1 hour in rear
        of 10th. Infantry Brigade and take up positions to defend the
        YELLOW LINE approximately as follows:-

            4 guns at Q.1.d.2.5.
            4 guns at Q.1.a.5.3. (R.1.A.5.2.)
            4 guns at P.6.b.5.3.
        4 guns will remain in support in BLUE LINE about P.12.a.

    (d) "B" Company will assemble in P.6. (Guns and belt boxes on
        limbers) and will move forward at Zero plus 1 hour in rear of
        11th. Infantry Brigade and take up positions to defend the
        YELLOW LINE approximately as follows:-

            4 guns at J.36.c.9.4.
            4 guns at J.35.d.5.9.
            4 guns at J.35.a.9.3.
        4 guns will remain in support in Blue Line about P.4.b.

                                                            P.T.O.

(2)

(e) "C" and "A" Companies will move from their present defensive positions to their barrage positions after dark on night 23/24th. October.

(f) On night 24/25th. inst "C" Company will be prepared to move to billets in VERCHAIN. "A" Company to billets in HASPRES. These Companies will not move until receipt of orders from Battalion Headquarters.

4. LIASON WITH INFANTRY BRIGADES

O.C."C" Company will remain at 10th. Infantry Brigade Headquarters until line is taken over by G.O.C. 12th. Infantry Brigade.
O.C."A" Company will remain at 11th. Infantry Brigade Headquarters until line is taken over by G.O.C. 12th. Infantry Brigade.
OC "D" and B Companies on capture of final objective will establish their headquarters in VERCHAIN.
O.C. "D" Company will be in close proximity to Headquarters 12th Infantry Brigade with which he will be connected by telephone

5. ZERO hour will be 4 a.m. 24th. October 1918.

6. ACKNOWLEDGE.

(sd) E.A. WILLIAMS Capt. & Adjutant
4th. Battalion Machine Gun Corps.

Distribution:-
Copy No. 1 O.C."A" Company
         2   "B"   "
         3   "C"   "
         4   "D"   "
         5   C.O.
         6   2nd. in Command.
         7   10th. Inf. Bde.
         8   11th. Inf. Bde.
         9   12th. Inf. Bde.
        10   4th. Division
        11   File
        12   File
        13   War Diary
        14   War Diary

Secret   Copy No

4th BATTN. MACHINE GUN CORPS INSTRUCTIONS FOR OFFENCE No 6

Ref: Sheet 51A.N.E. 1:20000.   28th Oct 1918

(1) General Plan

On a date & at a time to be notified later the 4th Division will attack & capture the Village of PRESEAU & the high ground to the North of the Village — The 11th Inf. Bde. will carry out the attack — The 61st Division will be attacking on the right — The 49th Division on the left.

(2) The Divisional Boundaries & Objective are shown on the attached Tracing.

(3) Detail of Action of Machine Guns

(a) Barrage Group. — O.C. Major Bennett — will consist of A & C. Companies & B Company 102nd M.G. Battn.
The Group from positions in K 27 & K 28 will place a barrage across the Divisional front from K.23.d.9.3. to MOULIN de SAMEON K 16 b 6 2.
Time Zero to Zero plus 15.
Rate of Fire 1 Belt in 5 Minutes
At Zero plus 15 these guns will lift on to Area K 18
Time of "Cease Fire" will be notified.
A Coy & B Coy 102nd Bn. will move from their present positions to their barrage positions after Dusk on Zero – Zero minus one night.

(b) D. Coy (Guns & belts on limbers) will assemble in K 26 c & will advance in close support of 11th. Inf. Bde. to positions approx. as shown on the attached Tracing.

(c) B. Coy. (Guns & belts on limbers) will assemble in K 25 d & will advance at Zero plus 60 & take up positions approx as shown on attached Tracing

(d) A Battalion Report Centre will be found in ARTRES. Location will be notified

(e) When Objective has been obtained B. Coy 102nd Battn will take up defensive positions on the Ridge West of ARTRES approx as follows. 3 Guns at K 28 a 3 6.
                           3 Guns at K 22 6 3 9.

(f) On Zero, Zero plus one night A & C. Coys' will be withdrawn to Billets – probably in Vicoigne.

4. Acknowledge.

                                    (Sgd) E.A. WILLIAMS. Capt & Adjt
                                           4th Battn. M. G. Corps.

Secret

Addendum No. 1. to 9th Bn. M.G.C.
Instructions for Offence No. 6.

Oct. 31st. 1918

1) The probable direction of hostile counter-attacks appear to be from:— (A) The village of SAULTAIN with a view to regaining the high ground in K.11. K.12.&L.7.

or (B) The direction of CURGIES or SEBLAIN to regain the village of PRESEAU and the high ground in L.19 & K.29.

In any case it seems that any counter attacks against this Division will most probably fall on the junction with Flanking Divisions.

(2) Action of Machine Guns

(a) D Coy will push forward two guns to positions about L.13c.8.0. as soon as possible after the BLUE LINE is captured.

These guns will be sited with a view to bringing direct fire up the valley in L.19 c & d.

(b) On S.O.S. signal being sent up, four guns of D Coy. in L.19 a will put down a barrage on the S.W. edge of the FORT-de-CURGIES. from L.9d.30-18. to L.9c.9-5.

Eight guns of B Coy. from positions in K.24 c. & K.18 c. will put down a Barrage on high ground from L.13 a. 0. to L.19 b. 3-9.

(c) Should these guns be called upon to fire on S.O.S. lines a reserve of 4 belt boxes per gun must be maintained for direct fire.

3) Contact Planes

Contact Patrols will call for planes at:—

Zero + 1¾ hours
Zero + three hours
Zero + five hours.

Counter attack machines will be in the air all day.

E. Williams
Capt & Adj.
9th Battn M.G. Corps.

Issued at 15·15 hours.

CONFIDENTIAL

WAR DIARY

OF

4TH. BATTALION MACHINE GUN CORPS

FROM ..Nov..1st..1918... TO ..Nov..30th..1918...

(Volume IX)

[signature] Capt pp. Lt. Colonel,

Commdg. 4th. Battalion Machine Gun Corps.

WAR DIARY
or
INTELLIGENCE SUMMARY.
(Erase heading not required.)

Army Form C. 2118.

Place	Date	Hour	Summary of Events and Information	Remarks and references to Appendices
In field	1/11/18		The 11th Inf Bde attack in the morning. D Coy moved forward with the attacking infantry and B Coy were in close support. A and C Coy and B Coy B 102 Bn put down a barrage during the initial stages of the attack. D Coy at their assembly point came under very heavy shell fire which slightly disorganised them. Some casualties were sustained to mule and personnel which delayed the Coy moving forward. However they were able to get into action in time to break up a counter attack which came on Infantry out of the village of PRESEAU. The Company did very good work throughout the day.	Ewen
"	2/11/18		The attack was continued this morning and we succeeded in establishing our objective for the 11/11/18. D Coy moved forward to support the Infantry and B Coy sent forward 2 Guns to [struck] the South to cover the village of PRESEAU from the right by the 11th Bn on the night 2/3. The Armoured was relieved in the fields at VERCHAIN staging there for a few C Coy returns to billets at VERCHAIN and the returning to billet at AVESNES-LE-SEC Rooms and then returning	Ewen

Army Form C. 2118.

WAR DIARY
or
INTELLIGENCE SUMMARY.
(Erase heading not required.)

Instructions regarding War Diaries and Intelligence Summaries are contained in F. S. Regs., Part II. and the Staff Manual respectively. Title pages will be prepared in manuscript.

Place	Date	Hour	Summary of Events and Information	Remarks and references to Appendices
Sutrepuit	3/11		Early this morning Band Boys returned to billets in VERCHAIN where they stayed for a few hours then proceeded to AVESNES-LE-SEC. to not Billet. A Coy remained in position until 1000 hrs when they withdrew and returned to billets in AVESNES-LE-SEC. Advanced Bn HQrs closed at VERCHAIN at 1000 hrs.	Ean
"	4/11		Coys spent the day cleaning up, and checking all kit.	Ean
"	5/11		Cleaning and checking completed	Ean
"	6/11		Section Training	Ean
"	7/11		Section Training	Ean
"	8/11		Section Training	Ean
"	9/11		Platoon Company Training	Ean
"	10/11		Coy Training	Ean
"	11/11		Armistice was signed with enemy at 0500 hrs today and cease fire was ordered at 1100 hrs. Bn marched to SAULTAIN	Ean

Army Form C. 2118.

WAR DIARY
or
INTELLIGENCE SUMMARY
(Erase heading not required.)

Place	Date	Hour	Summary of Events and Information	Remarks and references to Appendices
In the Field	12/18		Company training was continued.	Ears
"	13/18		Company training. The C.O. inspected each company separately on their own parade ground. 2 hours a day is to be devoted to Educational training to assist men in returning to their civil occupation. Today the Classes were organised and instructors in the various subjects appointed.	Ears
"	14/18		Company Training from 0900hrs to 1100hrs. Educational Class 1130hrs to 1245hrs.	Ears
"	15/18		Battalion Route march 0900hrs to 1100hrs. Educational Class 1130hrs to 1245hrs.	Ears
"	16/18		Route march under Coy arrangements, & an inspection. Educational Class 1130hrs to 1245hrs.	Ears
"	17/18		Special units Church parade at PRESSEAU for Thanksgiving Service.	Ears

Army Form C. 2118.

WAR DIARY
or
INTELLIGENCE SUMMARY.
(Erase heading not required.)

Instructions regarding War Diaries and Intelligence Summaries are contained in F. S. Regs., Part II. and the Staff Manual respectively. Title pages will be prepared in manuscript.

Place	Date	Hour	Summary of Events and Information	Remarks and references to Appendices
Bethune	July 18/18		Bn. Route march from 0900 hrs to 11.00hrs. Education Classes from 11.30 to 12.45 hrs.	Ean.
"	19/18		Practice Ceremonial parade for the C.O.C.'s inspection. Education Class.	Ean.
"	20/18		The Divisional Commander, Maj. General CH. Indeal Lucas C.M.G. K.S.O. inspects the Division on the Aerodrome SAULTAIR.	Ean.
"			The Battalion moved to RONZIER BARRACKS VALENCIENNES during the afternoon.	
"	21/18		Parades under Company Arrangements. Class rooms for the Education were allotted and thoroughly cleaned out.	Ean.
"	22/18		The Barracks were found to be in a very dirty state and rooms were thoroughly cleaned out today.	Ean.
"	23/18		Education Classes 11.30 hrs to 12.45 hrs. The A.O.C. inspects the Bn. Transport on the line of march. Company training 0900 hrs to 11.00hrs. Education Class 11.30 to 12.45 hrs Football League have commenced matches. Played 9/8 in the afternoon.	Ean.

WAR DIARY
or
INTELLIGENCE SUMMARY.
(Erase heading not required.)

Army Form C. 2118.

Place	Date	Hour	Summary of Events and Information	Remarks and references to Appendices
In Field	24/11/18		Church Parade at Valenciennes Theatre.	Ees
"	25/11/18		Coy Training and Education Classes	Ees
"	26/11/18		Company Training and Education Classes. The following men awarded the Military Medal for gallantry and devotion to duty in the operation between Oct 20th 1918 and Nov. 2nd 1918. 67689 Co.m.S. Greenaway, 8778 A/Sergt N Jarvscath, 115792 A/Sgt Marwick 21128 Cpl J Green, 99805 Cpl W R Parkinson, 13386 L/Cpl J Birtwistle, 143094 Pte E Crippo, 68322 Pte C Checkfield, 133556 Pte Richards W.	Ees
"	27/11		Coy Training and Education Classes.	Ees
"	28/11		The Army Commander inspected the Division on the Aerodrome at SAULTAIN. Forty files per Coy were on parade and no transport.	Ees
"	29/11		Company Training and Education Classes	Ees
"	30/11		Weekly Inspection of Barrack Rooms and Kit. Education Classes.	Ees

CASUALTIES NOVEMBER.

Nov.1 Lieut. Gingell.L.V.H. Wounded Gas
       "   Allen. H.G.   wounded
       25 other ranks wounded
       4   "   "   Hospital

2   2/Lieut. H.W.Phillips. wounded, Gas
       "   P.S.Butterworth. "
       76 other ranks wounded Gas.
       10   "   "   wounded
       3   "   "   killed
       33   "   "   reinforcements

3   Major E.C.Rands reinforcement
       Lieut. A.E.Ward.

4.   2/Lieut. B.G.John to hospital
       5 other ranks   "

5.   Lieut. T.Pratt reinforcement
       2 other ranks to hospital

6.   Lieut. Filmore reinforcement
       66 other ranks reinforcements
       4   "   "   to hospital

7.   Lieut. J.P.Runciman to 15th. Battl. M.G.C.
       2/Lieut. F.R.Payne MC to R.A.F.
       Lt. Col. Somerville to hospital
       Lieut. L.J.Fuller to hospital
       3 other ranks to hospital

8.   2/Lieut. Ingham
       "   Stamp
       "   Fitzgerald
       "   Pook.
       20 other ranks reinforcements.

8.   Capt. S.Bartlett.)
       "   S.G.Sim.   ) to M.G. School G.H.Q.
       6 o.R.s   )
       4 other ranks to hospital

9.   Lt. Col. Somerville rejoined
       4 other ranks to hospital

10.   2/Lieut. W.B.Moor to hospital
       2 other ranks to hospital

11   NIL

12.   6 other ranks reinforcements
       1   "   "   to hospital

13.   22 other ranks reinforcements
       6   "   "   to hospital

(2).

14.	Major Hodgson Rejoined 8 other ranks to hospital
15	5 other ranks to hospital
16.	Capt. S.Bartlett) " S.G.Sim) rejoined from course M.G. School. 6 other ranks) 4 other ranks to hospital

17	Lieut. Gay)
	  " Davies R.D.)
	  " Winchcombe) reinforcements
	44 other ranks)
	3 other ranks to hospital

18	2/Lieut. Haslam reinforcement " A.C.Drew to hospital 2 other ranks "
19.	4 other ranks to hospital
20.	7 other ranks to hospital
21	Lieut. Hewitt reinforcement " Holme " 4 other ranks to hospital
22	2/Lieut .Lorimer reinforcement 41 other ranks " 2 " " hospital 1 " " to U.K.
23	2/Lieut. Filmore First Army School 2 other ranks " 3 other ranks to hospital
24	1 other rank reinforcement 4 " " hospital
25	3 other ranks hospital
26	4 other ranks to hospital
27	3 other ranks to hospital
28	21 other ranks reinforcements.
29	1 other rank reinforcement 4 " " hospital
30	1 other rank to hospital

S E C R E T.
==================

To:- 4th Division "A"

                Herewith original of War Diary for the month of December 1918.

                                      Ewilliam Capt.

5/1/19.   for. Lieut. Colonel,
                Commanding 4th. Battn. Machine Gun Corps.

4TH BATTALION
MACHINE GUN
CORPS
No. 2/394
5/1/19

ORIGINAL.

4th. Battalion Machine Gun Corps.

W A R   D I A R Y.
****

Period:- DECEMBER 1st. 1918. to DECEMBER 31st. 1918.

SECRET

WAR DIARY
or
INTELLIGENCE SUMMARY.
(Erase heading not required.)

Army Form C. 2118.

Place	Date	Hour	Summary of Events and Information	Remarks and references to Appendices
In the Field	1/9/18		Bn. Church Parade.	Ears.
Valenciennes	2/9/18		Bn. training – Company arrangements.	Ears.
	3/9/18		Bn. training – Education Class.	Ears.
	4/9/18		Bn. training – Education Class.	Ears.
	5/9/18		Application practice – bn. fired at 400 x Range by all companies.	Ears.
	6/9/18		Bn. training – Ceremonial Drill – Education Class.	Ears.
	7/9/18		Inspection and Barrack room Cleaning. The G.O.C. 4th Division inspected the Bn. Transport on the Barrack Square at 1000 hrs. The turnout was clean and very good.	Ears.
	8/9/18		Church parade at Valenciennes Theatre at 1000h.	Ears.
	9/9/18		Parade. B. & C. Coys. Tactical Exe. A & D Coy. Close Order Drill – Lewis-gun / Arms, Exe. Drill. Education Classes for Whole Bn.	Ears.

WAR DIARY or INTELLIGENCE SUMMARY

Army Form C. 2118.

Place	Date	Hour	Summary of Events and Information	Remarks and references to Appendices
Valenciennes	10/11/18		Bn Training. Education Class. The afternoon games to Maidens held for Champions Gallantry in taken near Preseau on Nov 1st 1918. 66709 Sgt England E. 61/28 Pte Coombs W.	Eaw.
	11/11/18			Eaw.
	12/11/18		Bn Route March - Education Class	Eaw. Eaw.
	13/11/18		Bn Training. Education Class. Bn Training - Education Class. The shoulder title MGC only will be worn, the MGC will not be worn in future.	Eaw. Eaw.
	14/11/18		Weekly Inspection of Interior Economy - Education Class. Eaw.	
	15/11/18		Church Parade - Valenciennes theatre took.	Eaw.

WAR DIARY
or
INTELLIGENCE SUMMARY.
(Erase heading not required.)

Army Form C. 2118.

Place	Date	Hour	Summary of Events and Information	Remarks and references to Appendices
Valenciennes	16/12/18		Bn Training – Ceremonial Drill – Education Classes.	Env.
	17/12/18		Bn Training – Education Classes. The demobilisation has commenced and Coal miners are being despatched to disposal station – N.K. Returns home – the Coal mines – U.K. Returns home to work – One party left on the Bn on the 13th inst and another party leaves to-day. Full nominal list attached.	Env. Env.
	18/12/18		Bn Training – Route March – Education Classes.	Env.
	19/12/18		Bn Training – Education Classes. The Afternoons are devoted to Sport. The Bn have also a team entered in the Divisional Cup tie for the Kuwan Challenge Cup, and a Rugby team for the Divisional Championship. In addition there is now inter section championship running in the Bn.	Env.

WAR DIARY
or
INTELLIGENCE SUMMARY.

(Erase heading not required.)

Army Form C. 2118.

Place	Date	Hour	Summary of Events and Information	Remarks and references to Appendices
Valenciennes	20/12/18		Bn. Tactical Exercise – Rear Guard action.	Ens.
	21/12/18		Weekly inspection and Scheme Economy. Bn. Co. Operation team won the rifle section competition (Alnerhuad) and 104 section H.Coy were runners up. (Bronze Medals).	Ens.
	22/12/18		Church Parade. Valenciennes Theatre.	Ens.
	23/12/18		Bn. Training. – Range practice 300 x 9400' range.	Ens. Ens.
	24/12/18		Parades and Coy. arrangements.	Ens.
	25/12/18		An excellent dinner of Turkey & Xmas pudding provided from canteen funds. The Bn. in various recreation & decorated, & the men thoroughly enjoyed the action.	Ens.
	26/12/18		Boxing Day. –	Ens.

Army Form C. 2118.

WAR DIARY
or
INTELLIGENCE SUMMARY.
(Erase heading not required.)

Instructions regarding War Diaries and Intelligence Summaries are contained in F. S. Regs., Part II. and the Staff Manual respectively. Title pages will be prepared in manuscript.

Place	Date	Hour	Summary of Events and Information	Remarks and references to Appendices
Valenciennes	27/12/18		Bn Training – Route March. Education Class	Ew.
	28/12/18		Weekly Inspection. Interior Economy. Education Class	Ew.
	29/12/18		Church Parade – Valenciennes Theatre looks Ea.	
	30/12/18		Bn Training. Ceremonial Drill. Education Class.	Ew.
	31/12/18		Bn Training – Route March – Education Class.	Ew.

CASUALTIES. DECEMBER 1918.

Dec. 1.   1 O.R. to Hospital.

    2.   2 O.R. to hospital.

    3.   2 O.R. to hospital.

    4.   11 O.R. to hospital.

    5.   6 O.R. to hospital.
            1 O.R. reinforcement.

    6.   5 O.R. to hospital.

    7.   Nil.

    8.   Q O.R. to hospital.
            2 O.R. reinforcements.

    9.   3 O.R. to hospital.

    10.   Nil.

    11.   Q O.R. to hospital.
            15 O.R. reinforcements.

    12.   1 O.R. to hospital
            2 O.R. to U.K. for Tour of Duty.

    13.   1 O.R. to hospital.
            2/Lt. Fitzgerald. R.V.L. to hospital.
            9 O.R. to U.K. for dispersal.

    14.   2 O.R. to hospital.

    15.   1 O.R. to hospital.
            20 O.R. reinforcements.

    16.   2 O.R. to hospital.
            3 O.R. reinforcements.

    17.   17 O.R. to U.K. for dispersal.

    18.   9 O.R. to U.K. for dispersal.

    19.   2 O.R. to hospital.

20.   1 O.R. to hospital.

21.   Nil.

22.   1 O.R. to hospital.
        15 O.R. to U.K. for dispersal
        2 O.R. reinforcements.

23.   2 O.R. to U.K. for dispersal.
        47 O.R. reinforcements.

24.   1 O.R. to hospital.

25.   6 O.R. to U.K. for dispersal.

26.   1 O.R. to U.K. for dispersal.

27.   2 O.R. to hospital.
        1 O.R. reinforcement.

28.   1 O.R. to hospital.
        13 O.R. to U.K. for dispersal.

29.   1 O.R. to hospital.
        Major E.C. Rands to 29th. Battn.M.G.C.
        1 O.R. to U.K. for dispersal.

30.   2 O.R. to hospital.
        1 O.R. to Watford.
        ½ O.R. to U.K. for dispersal.

31.   1 O.R. to hospital.

ORIGINAL.

4TH. BATTALION MACHINE GUN CORPS.

WAR DIARY.

Period:- JANUARY 1ST. 1919 to JANUARY 31ST. 1919.

SECRET.

Army Form C. 2118.

WAR DIARY
or
INTELLIGENCE SUMMARY.
(Erase heading not required.)

Instructions regarding War Diaries and Intelligence Summaries are contained in F. S. Regs., Part II. and the Staff Manual respectively. Title pages will be prepared in manuscript.

Place	Date	Hour	Summary of Events and Information	Remarks and references to Appendices
Lt. Guds.	1/1/19		New Year's day. — No parade for R. Lists + ccommunity fun was any gr.	Ers.
"	2/1/19		Battalion training.	Ers.
"	3/1/19		Battalion training. Regimental Cmdship of Bth discontinued.	Ers.
"	4/1/19		Interior economy and Inspection.	Ers.
"	5/1/19		Church parade at Valenciennes 10 o'c.	Ers.
"	6/1/19		The Bn moved to Audeplin by Bus. Billets found for practically every man in the Bn and also provided for Coy arrangements.	Ers.
"	7/1/19		Parades under Coy arrangements.	Ers.
"	8/1/19		Bn training.	Ers.
"	9/1/19		Bn training.	Ers.

A7092). Wt. w1185/9/M1297. 750,000. 1/17. D. D & L., Ltd. Forms/C2118/14.

WAR DIARY
INTELLIGENCE SUMMARY

Army Form C. 2118.

Place	Date	Hour	Summary of Events and Information	Remarks and references to Appendices
Anderlue	10/19		Bn training.	Ens.
	11/19		Weekly inspection. Gas Brick, etc.	Ens.
	12/19		Church parade.	Ens.
	13/19		Bn training	Ens.
	14/19		Bn training	Ens.
	15/19		Bn training	Ens.
	16/19		Bn training. The final for the Queens Cup was played today at La Louvière. The Bn were beaten by 1st 2 Essex Bn by 3 goals to nil. Lt Noble the Capt of the Bn team was accidentally injured. (broken nose).	Ens.
	17/19		Bn training.	Ens.
	18/19		Billet and kit inspection	Ens.

Army Form C. 2118.

WAR DIARY
or
INTELLIGENCE SUMMARY.
(Erase heading not required.)

Instructions regarding War Diaries and Intelligence Summaries are contained in F. S. Regs., Part II. and the Staff Manual respectively. Title pages will be prepared in manuscript.

Place	Date	Hour	Summary of Events and Information	Remarks and references to Appendices
Anderlues	19/19.		Church parade.	Ens
	20/19.		Bn Route march	Ens
	21/19.		Bn training	Ens
	22/19.		Bn training	Ens
	23/19.		Bn training	Ens
	24/19.		Bn training	Ens
	25/19.		Manoeuvre & inspection	Ens
	26/19.		Church parade.	Ens
	27/19.		Bn Route march.	Ens
	28/19.		Battalion training	Ens
	29/19.		Battalion training	Ens
	30/19.		Battalion training	Ens

Army Form C. 2118.

WAR DIARY
or
INTELLIGENCE SUMMARY.
(Erase heading not required.)

Instructions regarding War Diaries and Intelligence Summaries are contained in F. S. Regs., Part II. and the Staff Manual respectively. Title pages will be prepared in manuscript.

Place	Date	Hour	Summary of Events and Information	Remarks and references to Appendices
Bns Bn	31.10.19		Bn training. List of Casualties during the month is attached.	Enc. Enc.

Anderlues

CASUALTIES. JANUARY 1919

Jan. 1.	1 O.R. to hospital.		Jan 23.	1 O.R. To hospital.
2.	1 O.R. to hospital. 1 O.R. Reinforcement. 6 O.R. To U.K. for dispersal.		24.	Lieut. Pratt. & 14 O.R. for dispersal.
3.	2 O.R. To hospital. 1 O.R. Reinforcement. 1 O.R. To Dispersal Station U.K.		25.	2 Reinforcements. Lieut. Stevens. & 14 O.R. for Dispersal.
4.	1 O.R. To hospital. 2 O.R. Reinforcements.		26.	Capt. Bartlett. & 14 O.R. for Dispersal.
8.	1 O.R. To hospital.		27.	Lieut. Bond. & 19 O.R. for Dispersal.
9.	1 O.R. To hospital. 2/Lt. H.W. Phillips.& 32 O.R. Reinforcements.		28.	Lieut. Cruickshank.& 19 O.R. for Dispersal.
10.	9 O.R. To U.K. for Dispersal.		29.	1 O.R. To hospital. 4 O.R. reinforcements.
11.	13. O.R. To U.K. for dispersal.		31.	1 O.R. To hospital. Lieut. Holme. & 12 O.R. for dispersal.
12.	13 O.R. To U.K. for dispersal.			
13.	1 O.R. reinforcement. 13 O.R. for dispersal.			
14.	1 O.R. reinforcement. Capt. Sim & 4 O.R. to U.K. for Dispersal.			
16.	Lieut. Holme & 2 O.R. to hospital.			
18.	1 O.R. Reinforcement.			
19.	Lieut. Hughes. & 14 O.R. to U.K. for Dispersal.			
20.	14 O.R. to U.K. for Dispersal.			
21.	2 O.R. to hospital. 2 O.R. reinforcements. Lieut. Gay. & 14 O.R. to U.K. for Dispersal.			
22.	1 O.R. to hospital. Lieut Holme from hospital.			

Vol 13

ORIGINAL.

4th BATTALION MACHINE GUN CORPS.

WAR DIARY.

FEBRUARY, 1919.

SECRET.

Army Form C. 2118.

WAR DIARY
or
INTELLIGENCE SUMMARY.
(Erase heading not required.)

Place	Date	Hour	Summary of Events and Information	Remarks and references to Appendices
Aueulue	1/7/19		No parades. 4th Divisional Routine Order No 3345 by Maj. General L.H. Findall Lucas CMG DSO. Infantrie reformment will be held on Saturdays. No parents report to fatigues.	Ean
	2/7/19		Church parade	Ean
	3/7/19		Company parades (movements being too severe for a Battalion)	Ean
	4/7/19		Battalion Training	Ean
	5/7/19		Battalion Training	Ean
	6/7/19		Battalion Training	Ean
	7/7/19		Battalion Training	Ean

Army Form C. 2118.

WAR DIARY
or
INTELLIGENCE SUMMARY.
(Erase heading not required.)

Instructions regarding War Diaries and Intelligence Summaries are contained in F. S. Regs., Part II. and the Staff Manual respectively. Title pages will be prepared in manuscript.

Place	Date	Hour	Summary of Events and Information	Remarks and references to Appendices
Auderlues	8/9		No parade	Ean
	9/9		Church parade	Ean
	10/9		Battalion Route March	Ean
	11/9		Battalion Training	Ean
	12/9		Battalion Training	Ean
	13/9		Battalion Route March	Ean
	14/9		Battalion Training. To ensure safekeeping all holdings not being called in from Coys and stores to be in Ordn Stores. 4 Battalion 450 ORs detailed proceed to South Bn H.Q. to be held in readiness to proceed on receipt of further orders.	Ean
	15/9		No parade. Demobilization of officers ceased except for those released prior to G.A.O.14 29/11/19.	Ean
	16/9		Church Parade	Ean

WAR DIARY
or
INTELLIGENCE SUMMARY.
(Erase heading not required.)

Army Form C. 2118.

Place	Date	Hour	Summary of Events and Information	Remarks and references to Appendices
Anderlue	17/2/19		Training under Coy arrangements.	En
	18/2/19		Training under Coy arrangements	En
	19/2/19		All available paraded for instruction under RSM.	En
	20/2/19		Training under Coy arrangements. All leave to UK stopped except in case of men returned as volunteers for K Army of Occupation.	En
	21/2/19		Reduction in transport drivers has made it very difficult to maintain efficiency. All available men with Bn were detailed to work on cleaning harness and all transport material.	En
	22/2/19		Parade under Coy arrangements.	En
	23/2/19		Church parade.	
	24/2/19		Parades under Coy arrangements.	

Army Form C. 2118.

WAR DIARY
or
INTELLIGENCE SUMMARY.
(Erase heading not required.)

Instructions regarding War Diaries and Intelligence Summaries are contained in F. S. Regs., Part II. and the Staff Manual respectively. Title pages will be prepared in manuscript.

Place	Date	Hour	Summary of Events and Information	Remarks and references to Appendices
— Anderlues —	25/19		Parade unit Coy arrangements	Ens
	26/19		Parade unit Company arrangements	Ens
	27/19		The C.O. inspected the Bn by Companies. Dress "In K. field" is to be discontinued from today in all official documents in which it has hitherto been used, and the actual name of Khaki place will henceforward be used.	Ens
	28/19		Parade unit Coy arrangements	Ens
			List of casualties for the month is attached.	Ens

CASUALTIES - FEBRUARY 1919.

Feb. 1. 13 O/Rs to U.K. for
          Dispersal.
    2/Lt. Haslam F. to U.K.
         for Dispersal.

2. 3 O/Rs to Hospital.
   2 O/Rs reinforcements.
   10 O/Rs to U.K. for
         Dispersal.

3. 2/Lt. J.F. Clapham to hospital

5. 1 O/R to hospital.
   1 O/R reinforcement.
   2/Lt. Longland and
     13 O/Rs to U.K. Dispersal.

6. Lt. T. Smallwood and 20/Rs
     to hospital.
   1 O/R reinforcement.
   2/Lt. Lorimer D. and
     12 O/Rs to U.K. Dispersal

7. 2/Lt. Gowans, A.D. and
     14 O/Rs to U.K. Dispersal.

8. 20 O/rs to U.K. for Dispersal

9. 2/Lt. Ingham and 12 O/Rs
     to U.K. for dispersal.

10. 1 O/R to hospital.

11. 1 O/R to hospital.

12. 2/Lt. Jagoe A.W. & 13 O/Rs
     to U.K. for Dispersal.
    3 O/Rs to hospital.

13. 2 O/Rs to Hospital.
    2 O/Rs reinforcements.
    Lt. F.J. Stone and 13 O/Rs
     to U.K. for Dispersal.

14. 12 O/Rs to U.K. for Dispersal

Feb. 15. 1 O/R reinforcement.
     7 O/Rs to U.K. for dispersal.

16. 1 O/R to hospital.
    11 O/Rs to U.K. for dispersal

17. 1 O/R to hospital.

18. 2/Lt. F.N. Filmore to hospital
     and rejoined.

19. 8 O/Rs to U.K. for dispersal

20. 1 O/R to hospital.
    1 O/R reinforcement.
    11 O/Rs to U.K. for
        dispersal.

21. 1 O/R reinforcement.
    11 O/Rs to U.K. for
        dispersal.

22. 10 O/Rs to U.K. for
        dispersal.

23. 10 O/Rs to U.K. for
        dispersal.

26. 10 O/Rs to U.K. for dispersal.

28. 2 O/Rs to hospital.
    13 O/Rs to U.K. for dispersal

www.ingramcontent.com/pod-product-compliance
Lightning Source LLC
Chambersburg PA
CBHW051527190426
43193CB00045BA/2223